Andreas J. Obrecht (Hrsg.)

Wissen und Entwicklung III

Texte des Österreichischen
Nachwuchspreises für
Entwicklungsforschung 2015 und 2017
Mit einem einleitenden Essay zu
Armutsreduktion und sozialökologischen
Transformationen

StudienVerlag

Innsbruck
Wien
Bozen

Das Cover zeigt die Übersetzung des Ausschreibungstextes des Nachwuchspreises 2017 auf Dzongkha – der Nationalsprache Bhutans – von Langa Tenzin und Tshering Pelden, bei denen wir uns herzlich bedanken. Der deutsche Wortlaut ist:

„Was nachhaltiger Tourismus für Entwicklung alles kann bzw. nicht kann. Forschungen und wissenschaftliche Analysen und Ideen zu den entwicklungspolitischen Potentialen des nachhaltigen Tourismus."
Nachhaltiger Tourismus für Entwicklung wird als Förderer des interkulturellen Verständnisses und Dialoges angesehen, als ressourcenschonende Alternative zu Massentourismus, als Armut reduzierender und lokale Märkte positiv stimulierender ökonomischer Faktor sowie als Bewahrer des kulturellen Reichtums einer Region, eines Landes. In vielen wichtigen Dokumenten und Protokollen wird auf die Bedeutung und auch die Potentiale des nachhaltigen Tourismus für Entwicklung verwiesen.
Doch vermag es der nachhaltige Tourismus – insbesondere in Ländern des globalen Südens – tatsächlich, die vielfältigen Erwartungen zu erfüllen, die in ihn gesetzt werden? Oder wird hier alter Wein in neue Schläuche gegossen? Was trägt die Entwicklungsforschung zu einer realistischen Einschätzung der entwicklungspolitischen Möglichkeiten des nachhaltigen Tourismus bei? Und wie lassen sich theoretische Konzepte in der Praxis umsetzen?

© 2018 by Studienverlag Ges.m.b.H., Erlerstraße 10, A-6020 Innsbruck
E-Mail: order@studienverlag.at
Internet: www.studienverlag.at

Buchgestaltung nach Entwürfen von himmel. Studio für Design und Kommunikation, Innsbruck / Scheffau – www.himmel.co.at
Satz: Da-TeX Gerd Blumenstein, Leipzig
Umschlag: Eva Müllner und Werner Fulterer
Umschlagmotiv: globe-312668_1280 Pixabay/Clker-Free-Vector-Images
Englische Korrekturen: Jamie McDonald
Ko-Editorin: Alexandra Grieshofer

Gedruckt auf umweltfreundlichem, chlor- und säurefrei gebleichtem Papier.

Bibliografische Information der Deutschen Nationalbibliothek
Die Deutsche Nationalbibliothek verzeichnet diese Publikation in der Deutschen Nationalbibliografie; detaillierte bibliografische Daten sind im Internet über <http://dnb.dnb.de> abrufbar.

ISBN 978-3-7065-5915-7

Inhalt

Ruth Kutalek

Vorwort

Im schwedischen Film „The Square" wird ein urbanes Kunstobjekt eines argentinischen Soziologen und Künstlers vor ein Kunstmuseum platziert – ein quadratisch umrahmter Platz von einigen Quadratmetern innerhalb dessen alle Menschen die gleichen Rechte und Pflichten haben. Ein einfaches Viereck wird aus Licht gestaltet – ein „sanctuary of trust and caring". Was als Kunstobjekt beginnt, endet im Film in witzig-beißender Kritik am Kunstbetrieb, an der Migrationspolitik und an der Verlogenheit und Bequemlichkeit der Privilegierten. Was aber, wenn wir den fiktiven Künstler im Film beim Wort nähmen? Was, wenn unser Arbeitsplatz, unsere Nachbarschaft, der Ort, in dem wir leben, so ein „Square" wäre, in dem jede/r gleiche Rechte und Pflichten hat? Eine „Zufluchtsstätte von Vertrauen und Fürsorge"? Was müsste sich ändern? Wo würden wir beginnen? Wer würde diese Entscheidungen treffen und wie würden diese getroffen werden? Und wie würden wir unsere Umwelt in diese Überlegungen einbeziehen?

Im Prinzip sind die Sustainable Development Goals (SDGs) eine Aufforderung, die Welt so einem idealen Raum anzunähern. Wie sehen aber diese großen Ziele „Armut beenden, Ernährung sichern, gesundes Leben für alle, Bildung für alle, Gleichstellung der Geschlechter, Ungleichheit verringern; Frieden, Gerechtigkeit und starke Institutionen", die uns durch die SDGs vorgegeben werden, in der Realität der täglichen Praxis aus? Das sind Fragen, die nicht nur jede/r Einzelne von uns beantworten muss, sondern die auch strukturelle Mechanismen der Förderung erfordern.

Die Arbeit der Kommission für Entwicklungsforschung (KEF) und besonders der Österreichische Preis für Entwicklungsforschung, durch den entwicklungspolitisch relevante Forschung ausgezeichnet wird, ist ein Teil dieser strukturellen Mechanismen, über die die Erreichung der SDGs gefördert werden und die auch international ein wichtiges politisches Signal setzen. 1981 als direkte Folge der UN-Konferenz zu „Wissenschaft und Technologien für Entwicklung" gegründet, fördert die KEF die Entwicklungsforschung auf drei verschiedenen Ebenen: im Rahmen von wissenschaftlichen Projekten, als Thinktank für nationale und internationale Einrichtungen und in der Öffentlichkeitsarbeit. In dem hier vorliegenden Buch „Wissen und Entwicklung III" werden Texte von NachwuchsforscherInnen vorgestellt, die wissenschaftliche Erkenntnisse zu den Themen „nachhaltiger Tourismus" und „Stadtentwicklung" behandeln und die ein weites Spektrum an Reflexionen und entwicklungspolitisch relevanten Auseinandersetzungen aufspannen.

Entwicklungspolitik ist immer auch Demokratiepolitik und Frauenpolitik, das gilt nicht nur in den „Ländern des Südens", sondern auch in Europa und in Österreich. Es ist wichtig, aktiv gegen Ungleichheit, auch gegen Nationalismen und die Erosion der Demokratie aufzutreten, und dabei einfache und schnelle Antworten zu vermeiden, denn komplexe Sachverhalte brauchen Erklärungen und breites Verstehen von Zusammenhängen. Der Entwicklungsforschungspreis ist auch dafür geschaffen worden, stetig und persistierend immer wieder auf mögliche Änderungen hinzuweisen und „best-practice"-Beispiele und ungewöhnliche Lösungsansätze hervorzuheben. Insbesondere auch jungen Forscherinnen und Forschern wird so eine Plattform geboten, Ideen auszutauschen, eigene Forschungsarbeiten zu kommunizieren und Lösungsansätze einer interessierten Öffentlichkeit zugänglich zu machen.

Bei allen diesen Maßnahmen ist es essentiell, dass wir Diversität und multiple Meinungen zulassen, damit wir nicht Gefahr laufen, wie es die Schriftstellerin Chimamanda Ngozi Adichie ausdrückt, nur die eine Geschichte zu erzählen. Und so wird die eine Geschichte erzählt, „show a people as one thing, as only one thing, over and over again, and that is what they become". Im Kontext neuerer politischer Entwicklungen in Europa und Übersee ist das die gefährliche eine Geschichte die oft erzählt wird, von „Karawanen", „Wellen", „Bedrohungen" und „Illegalen". Globale Phänomene lassen sich aber mit solchen Politiken und Abschreckungs-Szenarien nicht lösen. Die KEF versteht sich auch hier als Teil der Zivilgesellschaft, die im Rahmen ihres öffentlichen Auftrages gegen eine solche „Normalisierung" wirkt, indem sie die größeren geopolitischen und ökonomischen Kontexte vermittelt. Die KEF macht Entwicklungspolitik und -forschung durch unterschiedliche Sichtweisen verstehbar, sodass nicht nur die eine Geschichte erzählt wird, sondern viele mögliche Geschichten, die zu der Realisierung eines nachhaltigen und friedlichen menschlichen Zusammenlebens beitragen.

Priv.-Doz. Mag. Dr. Ruth Kutalek
Vorsitzende des Kuratoriums der KEF

I   Einleitung

Andreas J. Obrecht

Armutsreduktion und sozialökologische Transformationen

Der Österreichische Preis für Entwicklungsforschung und die KEF

Jedes zweite Jahr vergibt die Kommission für Entwicklungsforschung (KEF) den „Österreichischen Preis für Entwicklungsforschung" aus Mitteln des Bundesministeriums für Bildung, Wissenschaft und Forschung (BMBWF). Der Hauptpreis wird für besondere Leistungen im Bereich der Entwicklungsforschung an Institutionen verliehen bzw. an Entwicklungsforscher/innen ad personam für ihr Lebenswerk.[1] Kriterien bei der Vergabe durch die Fachjury sind: wissenschaftliche Relevanz und Exzellenz, Bedeutung für Entwicklung, Beitrag zur Lösung „globaler Herausforderungen", Bedeutung für die Scientific Community und außerwissenschaftliche Öffentlichkeit. Der Nachwuchspreis würdigt wissenschaftliche Arbeiten, Artikel und Publikationen von an wissenschaftlichen Institutionen verankerten Post-Graduierten sowie von Post-Graduierten an ausländischen Institutionen, sofern sie österreichische Staatsbürger/innen sind, und wird nach denselben Kriterien wie der Hauptpreis verliehen. Der Nachwuchspreis wird thematisch ausgeschrieben, wobei es um die wissenschaftliche Darstellung, Analyse und um das Erarbeiten von Lösungskonzepten bezüglich „globaler Herausforderungen" im Sinne der Nachhaltigen Entwicklungsziele („Sustainable Development Goals", SDGs) geht.

Der vorliegende Reader enthält Texte, die zum Nachwuchspreis 2015 und 2017 eingereicht worden sind und zur Gänze den Siegerinnen-Text 2017. 2015 stand die Vergabe des Nachwuchspreises unter dem Motto: „Städte im Wandel. Entwicklung und Nachhaltigkeit der Städte im globalen Süden". 2017 wurde aufgrund des „International Year of Sustainable Tourism for Development" der Vereinten Nationen[2] folgende thematische Vorgabe getroffen: „Was nachhaltiger Tourismus für Entwicklung alles kann bzw. nicht kann. Forschungen und wissenschaftliche Analysen und Ideen zu den entwicklungspolitischen Potenzialen des nachhaltigen Tourismus."

Für die KEF stellt sich Entwicklungsforschung – im Einklang mit den nationalen und internationalen Diskursen zu Fragen der globalen Entwicklung und der sozialökologischen Transformationen – als transdisziplinäres Forschungsfeld dar,[3] dessen Ziel es ist, die Lebensbedingungen von definierten Populationen oder marginalisierten Gruppen in strukturschwachen Regionen und Ländern des globalen Südens nachhaltig zu verbessern und damit zum übergeordneten Ziel der

Armutsreduktion beizutragen.[4] Dieser transdisziplinäre Zugang ist zielgruppenspezifisch, lösungsorientiert und in den realisierten Forschungskooperationen partnerschaftlich und partizipativ organisiert. Die Themenbereiche sind vielfältig: Sie reichen von der Tropenmedizin und Malariaforschung über die Landwirtschaft, Urban Anthropology, Menschenrechte und Konfliktprävention, Nutztierforschung, Wasser- und Nahrungsmittelsicherheit etc. bis hin zu der Schaffung von spielerischen Freiräumen für Kinder in indischen Slums oder der Analyse von Verlaufsformen des Wissenstransfers.[5] In der Entwicklungsforschung geht es also einerseits um transdisziplinäre partnerschaftliche Zusammenarbeit zwischen Forschern und Forscherinnen aus den OECD Ländern und ihren Kollegen und Kolleginnen aus den Less und Least Developed Countries[6], mit dem Ziel der evidenzbasierten Verbesserung der Lebenssituation von durch Armut und Marginalisierung betroffenen Menschen, andererseits aber auch stets um die Generierung neuer Wissensräume, welche die Weiterentwicklung wissenschaftlicher Methodologien, Fragestellungen und auch die Implementierung der Ergebnisse grundsätzlich ermöglichen. Das ist ein spannender Anspruch, der an die Kreativität der Akteure in dem transdisziplinären Feld der Entwicklungsforschung hohe Ansprüche stellt.

Die Kommission für Entwicklungsforschung (damals noch für Entwicklungsfragen) wurde formell 1981 als österreichische Maßnahme nach der UN-Konferenz „Science and Technology for Development" an der Österreichischen Akademie der Wissenschaften eingerichtet und 2009 organisatorisch der OeAD-GmbH (Österreichischen Austauschdienst-Gesellschaft) angegliedert. Seit der Gründung der KEF konnten mehr als 100 Projekte in rund 40 Ländern durchgeführt werden, die einen wichtigen Beitrag zum wissenschaftlichen Verständnis von spezifischen Problemlagen in infrastrukturschwachen Gebieten darstellen und wichtige Anhaltspunkte und Lösungsvorschläge zur Verbesserung der Lebenssituation anbieten konnten.[7]

Armutsreduktion

Die KEF wird vom Bundesministerium für Bildung, Wissenschaft und Forschung finanziert, die Förderungen werden auf die österreichische „Official Development Assistance" (ODA) angerechnet, also auf die Mittel der staatlichen Entwicklungszusammenarbeit, die im Jahr 2017 rund 0,3 % des BNP betrugen.[8] Die prioritären Ziele der österreichischen Entwicklungspolitik werden im 2004 vom österreichischen Nationalrat verabschiedeten EZA-Gesetz in § 1 Absatz 3 folgendermaßen definiert: „1. die Bekämpfung der Armut in den Entwicklungsländern durch Förderung der wirtschaftlichen und sozialen Entwicklung, welche zu einem Prozess des nachhaltigen Wirtschaftens und des wirtschaftlichen Wachstums, verbunden mit strukturellem, institutionellem und sozialem Wandel führen soll, 2. die Sicherung des Friedens und der menschlichen Sicherheit, insbesondere durch die Förderung von Demokratie, Rechtsstaatlichkeit, Menschenrechten und guter Regierungsführung, sowie 3. die Erhaltung der Umwelt und der Schutz natürlicher Ressourcen als Basis für eine nachhaltige Entwicklung." Die thematischen Ausrichtungen aller KEF-Projekte lassen sich unter diesen prioritären Vorgaben subsummieren, die eine Bestätigung in den 2015 von den Vereinten Nationen beschlossenen Nachhaltigen Entwicklungszielen finden.

Wie ist es nun um die zentrale Herausforderung globaler Armutsreduktion bestellt? Als ich in die vierte Klasse Volksschule ging, realisierte ich allmählich, dass die Welt, in der ich lebte, offenbar extrem ungleiche Lebensbedingungen für ihre Bewohner und Bewohnerinnen bereithielt. Ich hörte von hunderten Millionen von Armen, die sogar massenhaft an Hunger starben, und ich hörte von den Reichen, die offenbar gar nichts zu tun brauchten, um einfach immer reicher zu werden. Die Idee eklatanter Ungerechtigkeit lag in der Luft – wie konnten Menschen verhungern, wenn andere in Luxus lebten? Die Idee der Ungerechtigkeit in der Welt wurde einerseits von der bemühten Volksschullehrerin geschürt, die den Kindern Grundzüge der Geografie und Weltwirtschaft näherzubringen versuchte, andererseits aber auch von einem engagierten kirchlichen Umfeld, in dem ich tätig war. Hunger und Reichtum hatten demnach auch noch einen anderen Aspekt: Denn eher ging ein Kamel durch das Nadelöhr, als dass ein Reicher in den Himmel kam![9]

Es war das Jahr 1970 als ich in die vierte Volksschulklasse ging – ein Jahr, das nach Meinung mancher Sozialwissenschaftler und Statistiker das schlimmste Jahr in der Geschichte der Menschheit war.[10] In diesem Jahr erreichte die weltweite Armut bislang ungekannte Ausmaße: 2,2 Milliarden Menschen lebten 1970 unter der „absoluten Armutsgrenze"[11] – das waren 60 % der damaligen Weltbevölkerung. Was damals nicht gewusst werden konnte, war freilich, dass das Jahr 1970 auch eine Trendwende markierte und ab diesem Jahr die globale Armut sukzessive sinken würde – und dies nicht nur prozentuell, sondern auch in absoluten Zahlen. Heute wird von rund 800 Millionen Menschen ausgegangen, die unter der absoluten Armutsgrenze leben, das sind bei rund 7,5 Milliarden Menschen im Jahr 2017 rund 10,7 % der Weltbevölkerung – ein Prozentsatz, der seit einigen Jahren gleichgeblieben ist. Enorme Fortschritte in der Armutsreduktion konnten vor allem seit den 1990er Jahren erzielt werden, die ambitionierten Ziele der 2000 in Kraft tretenden Millennium Development Goals (MDGs) konnten dabei bei weitem übertroffen werden:

> „The world attained the first Millennium Development Goal target – to cut the 1990 poverty rate in half by 2015 – five years ahead of schedule, in 2010. According to the most recent estimates, in 2013, 10.7 percent of the world's population lived on less than US$ 1.90 a day, that's down from 35 percent in 1990."[12]

Die hier referierten statistischen Daten beschreiben einen großen Erfolg und zugleich ein großes ethisches Dilemma.

Sinkende Wachstumsraten und ethisches Dilemma

Der Rückgang der extremen Armut hat vielerlei Gründe, die hier nicht analysiert werden können – verbesserte Grund- und Gesundheitsversorgung, medizinischer Fortschritt, Trickle-Down-Effekte durch volkswirtschaftliches Wachstum, Investitionen in Basisinfrastrukturen, Demokratisierung und Korruptionsabbau, massive Investitionen in Bildung und sinkende Fertilität – um nur einige zu nennen. All diese Bereiche wurden und werden von der internationalen Entwicklungszusammenarbeit in den ärmsten Ländern der Welt systematisch unterstützt. Und hier zeichnet sich auch statistisch gesehen der große Erfolg ab, wobei der sinkenden Fertilität eine Schlüsselrolle zukommt, denn sie ist Ursache und Folge systematischer Armutsbekämpfung.

Ich kann mich selbst noch erinnern als Mitte der 1980er Jahre für das Jahr 2000 9 Milliarden Menschen prognostiziert wurden, tatsächlich waren es etwas mehr als 6 Milliarden. Heute leben 7,5 Milliarden Menschen auf der Welt und vorsichtige Prognosen gehen davon aus, dass der zu erwartende „peak" 11,5 Milliarden nicht überschreiten wird, wobei dynamischere Prognosen errechnen, dass sich die Weltbevölkerung schon in den kommenden 30 Jahren bei maximal 9,5 Milliarden eingependelt haben wird.[13] Die sinkende Fertilität ist deshalb Ursache und Folge des globalen Wohlstandsgewinnes und der erfolgreichen Armutsreduktion, weil der höchst korrelierende Faktor für sinkende Fertilität überall die sinkende Kindersterblichkeit ist, und die zeigt wiederum ziemlich treffsicher an, ob und in welchem Ausmaß Menschen in Armut leben. Sinkt die Kindersterblichkeit in den ersten fünf Lebensjahren unter 10 %, so kann gemeinsam mit begleitenden Maßnahmen wie Bildung, Zugang zu Kontrazeptiven, Familienplanung etc. die Wachstumsrate signifikant gesenkt werden. Je weniger Kinder sterben, desto weniger Kinder müssen geboren werden, um die interfamiliale Unterstützung in armen Gesellschaften aufrechtzuerhalten.

Um diese Entwicklungen noch deutlicher zu exemplifizieren: Im 20. Jahrhundert hat sich die Menschheit verfünffacht – von 1,5 Milliarden um 1900 bis zu 7,5 Milliarden heute. Die globale Wachstumsrate ist in der ersten Hälfte des 20. Jahrhunderts förmlich explodiert und zwar von 0,8 % – ein Wert, der die Weltbevölkerung über einige Jahrtausende einigermaßen stabil hielt – auf 2,1 % im Jahr 1962. Wäre es bei diesem exponentiellen Wachstum geblieben – pro 100 Menschen kommen dabei pro Jahr statistisch gesehen 2,1 Menschen hinzu – müssten heute rund 11 Milliarden und um das Jahr 2030 schon 14 Milliarden Menschen auf unserem Planeten versorgt werden. Ein Horrorszenario, das nicht zu bewältigen ist. Heute liegt die globale Wachstumsrate bei 1,1 % – Tendenz sinkend.[14] Dass die absolute Zahl der Weltbevölkerung noch eine Zeit lang steigen wird liegt daran, dass die geburtenstarken Jahrgänge des 20. Jahrhunderts selbst für mehr Nachkommen gesorgt haben und dass die Lebenserwartung weltweit dramatisch gestiegen ist. 1950 belief sich die globale durchschnittliche Lebenserwartung bei Geburt auf 48 Jahre, heute auf 71,4 Jahre.[15] Die Alten dieser Welt fallen also immer später aus der Statistik heraus.

Obwohl sich im 20. Jahrhundert die Weltbevölkerung also verfünffacht hat, ist es gelungen den Anteil der extrem Armen an der Weltbevölkerung von 60 % auf

10,7 % zu reduzieren. Eine gigantische zivilisatorische Leistung, die viel Hoffnung auf eine sowohl sozial als auch ökologisch verträglichere Zukunft gibt.[16] Dennoch darf sich die Weltgemeinschaft nicht auf diesem Erfolg ausruhen. Die 800 Millionen Menschen, die heute noch unter der absoluten Armut leiden, stellen ein großes ethisches Dilemma dar, denn für einen extrem armen Menschen ist es völlig belanglos welchen Prozentsatz seine Existenzweise bezüglich der Lebensbedingungen der Mehrheit der Weltbevölkerung darstellt. Er leidet unter dieser Existenzweise und kann dieses Leid zumeist nicht einmal adäquat adressieren. In einer reichen, wohlhabenden, imperial über ihre Verhältnisse lebenden Welt stellt die Marginalisierung von 10,7 % der Weltbevölkerung – trotz der erzielten Erfolge – eine ethische Katastrophe dar.

Komplexe Zusammenhänge, partizipative Wissensräume und entwicklungspolitische Intervention

Mit moralischen Appellen – dazu auch noch später – ist freilich wenig auszurichten. Das gilt auch für die SDGs, die die Eliminierung der absoluten Armut bis 2030 ganz oben auf ihre Agenda gesetzt haben. Auch hier wird sich erweisen ob, wie und in welcher Intensität die Transformation normativer Zielvorgaben in politisches, gesellschaftliches Handeln und konkrete Maßnahmen gelingt. Dabei wird von besonderer Wichtigkeit sein, die Komplexität der Zusammenhänge zwischen sozialen, kulturellen, ökonomischen, technologischen und ökologischen Sphären analytisch zu ergründen. Die Entwicklungsforschung wird dabei ein wesentliches wissenschaftliches Instrumentarium sein, das evidenzbasierte Analyse und die Generierung lösungsorientierter Konzepte und deren Implementierung ermöglicht.

Schon die UN-Weltkonferenz Rio '92 hat unmissverständlich die Dependenz zwischen ökologischen und sozialen Problemfeldern thematisiert. Die dringlichen ökologischen Probleme – vom Klimawandel über das Artensterben bis hin zu der Verschmutzung der Weltmeere –, die sich seither dramatisch zugespitzt haben, sind nur gemeinsam mit den dringlichsten sozialen Problemen zu lösen. Solange extreme soziale Verwerfungen existieren, die ökonomischen Ungleichheiten zwischen Individuen, Stadt und Land, Nationen und ganzen Kontinenten stets größer werden und auch die noch bestehende extreme Armut nicht eliminiert ist, solange werden wir auch keine global lebensfördernden ökologischen Rahmenbedingungen schaffen können, die ein langfristiges Überleben der Menschheit sichern. Wir leben in unteilbaren, kommunizierenden Gefäßen. Der Epochenbegriff Anthropozän meint demnach auch, dass wir Menschen es sind, die das Schicksal des Planeten und unser Leben auf ihm in die Hände genommen haben und zwar sowohl im Konstruktiven als auch im Destruktiven. Das ist eine große Verantwortung, denn sie inkludiert die Möglichkeit zur Vernichtung gleichermaßen wie die Gestaltung einer Zukunft, der wir nicht plan- und hilflos ausgeliefert sind.

Die Gestaltung einer auf nachhaltiger Produktion und Reproduktion basierenden Zukunft bedarf neuer partizipativer Formen der Wissensproduktion und der Wissensanwendung. Jahrhundertelang war Wissen und Wissensvermittlung auch ein Instrument der Macht und der politisch-kolonialen Hegemonie. Partizipative Wissensproduktion kreiert neue Räume wechselseitigen Lernens und Erkennens, wobei epistemologische und methodologische Vielfalt jedenfalls gefragt ist. Nicht umsonst besinnt sich der Diskurs über zukunftstaugliche Lebensmodelle zusehends auf indigene Formen von Wissen. Der Vernetzung von Wissensbestandteilen wird in der Zukunft mehr Wert zugeschrieben sein, als der einzeldisziplinären Erkenntnis.[17]

Auch die Kommission für Entwicklungsforschung (KEF) betont immer wieder die, den von ihr geförderten Projekten zugrundeliegende inter- und transdisziplinäre Basis. Aber es ist nicht nur die thematische Durchdringung um die es da geht, sondern vor allem auch die Art und Weise wie – in oft ungewöhnlichen kulturellen und sozialen Kontexten – Wissen gewonnen wird. Gemeinsames Konzipieren, gemeinsames Forschen, gemeinsame Umsetzung der Forschungsergebnisse – immer denken und handeln in den KEF-Projekten Wissenschaftler/innen aus Österreich gemeinsam mit ihren Kollegen und Kolleginnen in den Partnerländern.

Bei diesen Projekten ist die Armutsbekämpfung zumeist kein unmittelbares, sondern ein mittelbares Ziel. Prioritär ist die Schaffung partizipativer Räume des Wissens auf Basis gemeinsamer Forschung, deren Ergebnisse in weiterer Folge in der einen oder in der anderen Art der Armutsbekämpfung, bzw. der Lösung ökologischer Herausforderungen zu Gute kommen sollen. Dabei müssen die gesellschaftlichen und auch politischen Rahmenbedingungen stets Berücksichtigung finden, denn die Ergebnisse praxisorientierter Forschung wollen auch in der konkreten sozialen Wirklichkeit realisiert sein. Oft ist das ein schwieriges Unterfangen – vor allem in Ländern, die von Hunger, Krieg, Migration und verschärften ökonomischen und politischen Instabilitäten geprägt sind. In solchen „Feldern" gestalten sich die wissenschaftlichen und forschungspraktischen Bedingungen zum Teil extrem schwierig. Aber auch diese Situationen bedingen neue Lernprozesse und Erfahrungen.

Auch bei den Themen des Nachwuchspreises für Entwicklungsforschung steht die Idee im Vordergrund, durch soziokulturell verträgliche Interventionen die ökonomische Basis der betroffenen Bevölkerungen nachhaltig zu verbessern – dies freilich auf evidenzbasierter Grundlage, die analytisches Verständnis gesellschaftlicher und technologischer Entwicklungen ebenso in sich vereint, wie einen vorsichtigen, nicht paternalistischen Zugang zur Generierung von spezifischen Lösungsansätzen. Dabei stellt sich stets die zentrale Frage, ob die Intervention überhaupt in der Lage sein wird, das angestrebte Ziel zu erreichen, welche erwünschten bzw. nicht erwünschten Effekte sie hat bzw. haben könnte. Bezogen auf den Preis 2017 lautet diese Frage etwa: Taugt Tourismus – und sei er noch so auf Nachhaltigkeit bedacht – überhaupt für eine kultursensitive und einigermaßen verteilungsgerechte Entwicklungsagenda? Die zentrale Frage, ob eine entwicklungspolitische Intervention zur Zielerreichung beiträgt, oder ob sie mehr zerstört als sie Positives zu bewirken imstande ist, lässt sich bei fast allen Projekten der Entwicklungszusammenarbeit stellen. Es ist Aufgabe der Entwicklungsforschung diese nicht immer leichte Risikoabschätzung auf Basis empirischer Befunde zu bewerkstelligen.

Grundsätzlich lässt sich sagen, dass die Entwicklungsforschung für jene, die über einen gewissen Abenteuergeist verfügen und über den eigenen disziplinären und kulturellen Tellerrand blicken, ein sicherlich spannendes und bereicherndes Forschungsfeld eröffnet. Kultur- und sprachüberschreitende Zusammenarbeit bezüglich herausfordernder Fragestellungen in sozialen Umwelten, die den europäischen oft diametral entgegengesetzt sind, verspricht jedenfalls Erkenntnisse, die nicht nur auf einer persönlichen Ebene sehr lehrreich sein können, sondern auch wissenschaftliche Dimensionen beinhalten, die in anderen Kontexten nicht oder nur bedingt auffindbar wären.

Die Verleihung des Nachwuchspreises und die Frage nach sozialökologischen Transformationen

Die Verleihung des „Österreichischen Preises für Entwicklungsforschung 2017" fand im Rahmen der 7. Österreichischen Entwicklungstagung statt, die die KEF gemeinsam mit anderen Organisationen unter der Leitung des Paulo Freire Zentrums mitorganisiert hat.[18] Am Eröffnungsabend gab es eine feierliche Zeremonie, bei der die Preisträger/innen geehrt und die Preise verliehen wurden.[19] Die Entwicklungstagung firmierte unter dem Titel: „Sozialökologische Transformationen jetzt!". Schon im Vorfeld der Tagung gab es heftige Diskussionen über unterschiedliche inhaltliche und auch ideologische Zugänge – insbesondere bezüglich der ökonomischen Bedeutung des privatwirtschaftlichen Sektors, aber auch global agierender Konzerne für die Beförderung oder Umsetzung der SDGs. Entwicklungspolitisch Interessierte und Engagierte halten in der Regel wenig von den Strategien global agierender Unternehmen – diese stehen eher als Symbol für die Verhinderung von gerechteren und sozialökologisch verträglicheren Gesellschaftsordnungen – sowohl im globalen Süden als auch im globalen Norden. In vielerlei Fällen keineswegs zu Unrecht.

Entwicklungspolitisch Interessierte rekrutieren sich in der Regel aus einer sozial engagierten Zivilgesellschaft, die auf exponentiellem Wachstum basierenden Ökonomien grundsätzlich eher skeptisch gegenübersteht. Auch hinsichtlich des UN-Jahres „Sustainable Tourism for Development" gab es im Vorfeld pointierte Kritik. „Nachhaltiger Tourismus" sei demgemäß nur ein weiteres Etikett, durch das sich die extrem ressourcenexploitierende und -verschleißende Tourismusindustrie ethisch zu legitimieren versucht.[20] Ungeachtet dieser zum Teil sicherlich berechtigten Einwände war es der KEF im Vorfeld dieser Tagung wichtig darauf hinzuweisen, dass ohne unternehmerische, kapitalistischer Logik folgende Investitionen in neue Basisinfrastrukturen, Technologien und Produkte keine weltweiten sozialökologischen Transformationen stattfinden werden. Mehr noch: Dass diese Transformationen schon längst begonnen haben und sich das nirgends deutlicher zeigt als in der Investitionspolitik vieler großer Unternehmen – sei es in der Substitution fossiler Energien durch erneuerbare, die die Energiewende bereits eingeleitet haben, sei es in neuen Mobilitätskonzepten oder in der Entwicklung smarter digitalbasierter Technologien, die auf Ressourcenschonung ausgerichtet sind und damit auch zu einer Dezentralisierung der Produktion und des Konsums und damit zu einer Reduzierung der Abhängigkeit von zentralistischen – technologischen und ökonomischen – Strukturen beitragen.

Geborgte Zeit und Staunen über die Produktivkraft des Kapitalismus

Aufgrund dieser Debatten und Überlegungen habe ich in Hinblick auf kapitalismuskritische Einwände mir wesentlich erscheinende Aspekte und Voraussetzungen für soziale Transformationen zusammengefasst, die ich hier kursorisch darstellen will.[21] Die Zukunftsfähigkeit der Organisation von Leben auf unserem Planeten – das ist für mich der wichtigste Aspekt der sozialökologischen Transformationen. Daraus folgt, dass sich Zeit nicht selbst auffressen darf! Seit Beginn der Industriellen Revolution haben wir Menschen begonnen auf Kosten der Zukunft zu leben, also Zeit und damit Ressourcen aus der Zukunft in die Gegenwart zu holen. Diese geborgte Zeit kann positive aber auch negative Konsequenzen haben: Positiv dann, wenn sinnvolle Investitionen in die Ermöglichung zukünftiger Leben getätigt werden – etwa durch Gesundheitsinfrastrukturen, die heute Geborene länger leben lassen. Negativ dann, wenn die falschen Investitionen zu einer Verschwendung von hinkünftigen Lebensverwirklichungsmöglichkeiten führen – etwa durch die Vernichtung der Biodiversität. Dann nämlich frisst sich die Zeit buchstäblich selbst auf!

Das, was das „kapitalistische Geldsystem" durch kreditierte Investition in der Realwirtschaft ermöglicht – also etwa Infrastrukturen „auf Pump" zu errichten – gilt natürlich auch für den Verbrauch beschränkter Ressourcen. Wir leben auf „Pump" – verbrauchen damit Zeit, die anderen nicht mehr zur Verfügung steht. Der „Earth Overshoot Day" ereignet sich von Jahr zu Jahr früher (in Österreich war dieser heuer schon am 13. April erreicht; global am 1. August 2018). Die Erschöpfung des Planeten wird also von Jahr zu Jahr größer und damit das Zeitfenster kleiner, das für global wirksames nachhaltiges Handeln offensteht.

Trotz oder gerade wegen dieser empirischen Erkenntnis staune ich wie ehedem Karl Marx über die enorme Produktivkraft des Kapitalismus und die daraus resultierende Beschleunigung der Entwicklung von innovativen Technologien. Mein Vater ist mit dem Pferdewagen im niederösterreichischen Horn gefahren, ich selbst habe meine Dissertation mit der Schreibmaschine geschrieben – heute lassen wir unsere Roboter den Mars erforschen und die quantenmechanische Datenübertragung bahnt sich als neueste Revolution in der digitalen Welt an. Von der Nanotechnologie bis zur Landung eines von Menschen gebauten Raumschiffes auf dem Saturnmond Titan kommen wir aus dem Staunen nicht mehr heraus. Ein Staunen wie und wodurch sich menschliches Denken und Hoffen materialisiert.

So wie heute folgten auch Technologieentwicklungen der Vergangenheit nicht in erster Linie dem frommen Wunsch „die Welt besser", sondern dem weniger frommen Wunsch „Kohle" im großen Stil zu machen. Jener, der die durch kapitalistische Technologieentwicklung entstandenen Gefahren und Ungerechtigkeiten beklagt – Atombombe, Ungleichheit, Hunger, Artensterben, Migration etc. –, trägt mit seinem Handy heute mehr komplexe Datenverarbeitungs- und -verknüpfungskapazitäten mit sich herum, als dem Kontrollzentrum in Houston bei den Apollo-Missionen zwischen 1961 und 1972 zur Verfügung standen. Viele Technologien haben zur Verheerung bzw. Verschmutzung des Planeten beigetragen, weil wir teilweise – wider besseren Wissens – die falschen, nämlich die destruktiven Technologien kommerziell betrieben haben – etwa Atom- und Kohlekraftwerke, Verbrennungsmotoren, mit Waffen bestückte Raketen etc.

Von der „sozialen" zur „ökologischen Frage"

Im Vorfeld der Österreichischen Entwicklungstagung – und natürlich auch in den vielen Foren und Workshops – wurde heftig die Frage diskutiert, ob die Priorität eher beim sozialen oder beim ökologischen Aspekt der Transformationen liegt oder liegen wird. Ich denke, dass die sozialökologischen Transformationen nicht ideologie- sondern technologiegetrieben sein werden – wie die meisten gesellschaftlichen Transformationen in der Geschichte der Menschheit. Wie oben beschrieben, wissen wir seit der UN-Weltkonferenz Rio '92, dass sich die Organisation der sozialen Sphäre nicht von der Organisation der ökologischen trennen lässt, aber der „Hebel" für die Transformation, oder modisch ausgedrückt der Narrativ, wird nicht die soziale Frage, sondern die „ökologische Lösung" sein.

Im Verlauf des 19. Jahrhunderts wurde die „soziale Frage" aufgeworfen. Nicht nur marxistischen Denkern wurde klar, dass der Kapitalismus sowohl enorme Technologie- und Produktivitätsschübe fabriziert, als auch ein Moloch, ein Untier ist, das seine innovatorische Stärke auf Kosten des Proletariats und der Menschen in den Kolonien entfesselt. Alle sozialen Bewegungen – von der Sozialistischen Internationalen bis hin zur katholischen Soziallehre – wollen dieses Untier domestizieren. Reformatoren wollen durch letztlich demokratisch legitimierte Gesetzgebung die destruktiven Auswirkungen des Kapitalismus – etwa durch Umverteilung – zügeln, bei gleichzeitigem Erhalt bzw. bei Erhöhung der Produktivkraft. Revolutionäre wollen den Kapitalismus abschaffen. Nur in den „realsozialistischen" Ländern wurde dieser Versuch gewagt, mit – wie ein Blick auf das 20. Jahrhundert zeigt – nicht nur unrühmlichen, sondern verheerenden Konsequenzen.

Kam die „soziale Frage", so wie wir sie verhandeln, im 19. Jahrhundert auf, so taucht die „ökologische Frage" Anfang der 1970er Jahre auf. Vorher gab es sie in unserem heutigen Sinne nicht. Das Problembewusstsein, dass die Welt und unser Leben in ihr ressourcenbegrenzt sind, hängt mit unserer nicht länger als zwei Generationen gewachsenen Vorstellung eines „blauen Planeten" zusammen, der als komplexes System zu schützen und für nachfolgende Generationen zu erhalten ist. Diese Vorstellung ist ebenfalls ein Produkt von Forschung und Technologie-entwicklung: von der Raumfahrt angefangen, die uns unsere Erde erstmals aus der Perspektive des Orbits, später aus schier unglaublicher Entfernung als verletzbar wirkendes, belebtes Pünktchen in einem undenkbar riesigen Kosmos zeigt, über die Erkenntnisse in der Biologie, Genetik, Kybernetik bis hin zu komplexen theorie-bestimmenden Simulationen von ökologischen Interdependenzen und Szenarien in systemanalytischen Modellen. Die Erkenntnisse der systemimmanenten ökologischen Begrenzung haben maßgeblich dazu beigetragen, dass die Notwendigkeit einer radikalen ökologischen Transformation ganz oben auf den (geo-)politischen Agenden steht. An stetig steigenden Ressourcenverbrauch gekoppeltes exponentielles Wachstum führt zwangsläufig zur Zerstörung der, dieses Wachstum ermöglichenden Systembedingungen. Wollen wir weiter von „Wachstum" reden – etwa im Sinne eines transformierten Wohlstandsbegriffes – so nur dann, wenn „Wachstum" von steigendem Ressourcenverbrauch entkoppelt ist.

Aller Kritik an der Konferenzrhetorik und an dem zögerlichen politischen Handeln zum Trotz meine ich, dass ein fundamentaler Paradigmenwechsel bezüglich der Wahrnehmung der Lebensbedingungen in unserer Welt, aufgrund eines vor nicht länger als maximal 60 Jahren erkannten Problems, eine große menschliche Leistung darstellt. Der Zug ist schon längst in Richtung dieses Paradigmenwechsels abgefahren. Kein Politiker, kein Staatsmann – mit Ausnahme Donald Trumps, dessen anachronistischer Kapitalismusbegriff im Nationalismus, Protektionismus und dem Technologieverständnis des 19. Jahrhunderts wurzelt – bezweifelt ernsthaft die Notwendigkeit der radikalen transformativen und damit zu einem Gutteil technologischen Umgestaltung, um den ökologischen Kollaps unseres Planeten zu verhindern. Die Dekarbonisierung der Wirtschaft – und damit der Mobilität, der Energiegewinnung, der Produktion von Industrie- und Verbrauchsgütern etc. – bis zum Ende unseres Jahrhunderts ist beschlossene Sache (G7-Gipfel-Beschluss-2015: 50 % – 70 % bis zum Jahr 2050, 100 % bis zum Jahr 2100). Wir stehen damit am Anfang eines gigantischen transformativen Experimentes, das enorme Investitionen in die Gegenwart und die unmittelbar bevorstehende Zukunft voraussetzt.

Enorme Investitionen und Technologieentwicklung

Um diese Herausforderung zu meistern, benötigen wir – mehr denn je – die geborgte Zeit. Aber für die richtigen Investitionen. Es sind enorme technologische und ökonomische Investitionen von Nöten, um die radikale Energiewende in den nächsten zwei Generationen zu realisieren. Und diese Investitionen haben bereits begonnen, sind im Begriffe nach altem kapitalistischen Muster die Welt umzugestalten, neue Märkte – auf denen Ideen, Waren, Dienstleistungen und Zukunftstechnologien gehandelt werden – zu erschließen. Grundlage der Massentauglichkeit „grüner Technologien" ist die digitale Revolution, die gerade dabei ist, ihren nächsten evolutionären Schritt zu vollziehen.

Mehr als die Hälfte der Weltbevölkerung lebt in Städten. In den vergangenen 120 Jahren sind die Städte und auch deren Peripherie rund um das Auto und dessen Verbrennungsmotor gebaut worden. Hat sich das Auto als ressourcenintensive Maschine seit mehr als hundert Jahren nicht grundsätzlich verändert, so ist es seit einigen Jahren zum technologischen Experimentierfeld zweier wesentlicher Bereiche geworden, ohne die ökologische Transformation nicht zu vollziehen ist. Smarte, sich selbst regulierende Systeme und CO_2-neutraler Schub. Beide Technologiefelder bedingen einander, obwohl sie ursächlich getrennt voneinander entwickelt wurden.

Die Industrielle Revolution baut auf fossiler Energieverwertung, Dampfmaschine, Mechanik und Tele(kabel)-Kommunikation auf. Politisch ist diese Ökonomie in den Strukturen des Nationalismus organisiert. Dazu gehören auch Waffenproduktion und immenser Ressourcenverschleiß. Die ökologische Transformation, die bereits begonnen hat, baut auf erneuerbarer Energie, Denkmaschinen, Kybernetik und digitaler Kommunikation auf. Politisch wird diese Ökonomie in einer ent-nationalisierten Welt Geltung erlangen können, weil die Technologien selbst grenzüberschreitend wirksam werden. Eine Verdichtung der (digitalen) Verkehrswege wird Protektionismus, Nationalismus und darauf basierende Hochrüstung ökonomisch anachronistisch werden lassen. Das, was wir heute erleben, ist ein „Backlash" – ein Aufflackern nationalistischer Strömungen und Politiken aufgrund der vielfältigen Formen der Globalisierung, die alle in Richtung multilateraler, überstaatlicher Regime und (Technologie)-Konventionen weisen.

Die „Richtungslosigkeit" des Kapitalismus

Der Kapitalismus als Produktivitätserhöhungs- und Gewinnmaximierungsstrategie ist richtungslos – davon bin ich überzeugt. Dem „Kapitalisten" ist es völlig gleichgültig, womit „Kohle" gemacht wird. Wenn die politischen Rahmenbedingungen geschaffen sind, die „Kohle" mit Öl zu machen, mit Waffenexporten oder mit desaströsen Produktionen in Billiglohnländern, dann wird das geschehen. Wenn die „Kohle" mit Windrädern, smarten Mobilitätssystemen, sauberen Produktionsbedingungen oder guten sozialen Standards – die sich etwa in den Aktienmärkten spiegeln – gemacht werden kann, dann wird in diese Felder investiert werden. Kapitalismus ist per se nicht destruktiv oder konstruktiv – er ist ein äußerst flexibles System, das auf sich verändernde Rahmenbedingungen nach gewinnorientierten Kriterien reagiert. Diese Rahmenbedingungen müssen – in einem radikal demokratischen Verständnis – von uns gesetzt werden. Wenn wir die „Falschen" wählen, dann dürfen wir uns nicht wundern, dass uns die politischen und auch sozialen Bewegungen gegen die Transformation noch eine Weile in Atem halten werden.

Das was als Lobeshymne auf die „Green Economy" erscheinen mag, ist die Einsicht in den einzigen ökonomischen Hebel, den wir aufgrund der enormen Investitionen, die zu tätigen sind, zur Verfügung haben. Normative Appelle sind begrüßenswert, werden aber die „neue Zeit" nicht anbrechen lassen. Sie ist bereits angebrochen, aufgrund technologischer Innovation, die unabsehbar viele neue

Märkte erschließen wird, die unternehmerische Gewinne und Wohlstandsgewinne versprechen. Interessant ist, dass sich diese Technologieschübe, wie oben angedeutet, teils unabhängig voneinander ereignen. Ein Beispiel dafür ist die Dezentralisierung der Energiegewinnung – eine egalitäre Utopie aus den 1970er Jahren. Das Einspeisen selbst produzierter erneuerbarer Energie – etwa durch Sonnenenergiegewinnung – in die Smart Grids, die sogenannten intelligenten Stromnetze und die gleichzeitige Möglichkeit der Entnahme von Energie aus dem Netz dann, wenn sie gebraucht wird, setzt sich selbst regulierende digital-kybernetische Systeme ebenso voraus, wie die Massentauglichkeit der Renewables. Beide Technologiefelder – ehedem getrennt voneinander entwickelt – werden derzeit großflächig zusammengeführt und verwirklichen – nach einem Jahrhundert gigantomanischer Großprojekte – die Möglichkeit, dass jeder sein eigener „Energieproduzent" und „-konsument" werden kann. Vor 40 Jahren noch völlig undenkbar.

Warum sieht das denn keiner?

Eine weitere Voraussetzung, dass es überhaupt Sinn macht, über sozialökologische Transformationen zu schreiben und eine Tagung darüber abzuhalten, ist der weiter oben ausführlich dargestellte, natürlich extrem ungleich verteilte, aber dennoch empirisch eindeutig feststellbare globale Wohlstandsgewinn. Und damit die sinkende Fertilität aufgrund sinkender Kindersterblichkeit. Das Ende des exponentiellen und auch linearen Bevölkerungswachstums, das Erreichen einer stabilen, oder besser noch sinkenden Weltpopulation zwischen 9,5 und maximal 11,5 Milliarden Menschen im Laufe dieses Jahrhunderts, sind die absolut notwendigen Voraussetzungen für die Sinnhaftigkeit sozialökologischer Transformationen, die auch lebenswerte Bedingungen für erst in vielen tausenden von Jahren geborene Menschen sicherstellen sollen und möglicherweise auch können.

Auch dieses Faktum verdanken wir der herrschenden – und das im doppelten Wortsinn – ökonomischen Ordnung auf unserem Planeten und der Tatsache, dass ökonomisches Wachstum – zwar in viel zu geringem Ausmaß aber doch – in Basisinfrastrukturen und Grundversorgungen fließt. Gäbe es diese ultimative Grenze des Weltbevölkerungswachstums nicht, hätten wir keine Chance, wir bräuchten auch keine Artikel mehr zu schreiben oder Konferenzen abzuhalten, denn die Konsequenz wäre entweder ein buchstäblich devastierter Planet, der Leben verunmöglicht, oder eine Eskalation von Gewalt im hobbesschen Sinn des „Homo homini lupus".

Pessimistische, um nicht zu sagen apokalyptische Szenarien erfreuen sich gerade heute wieder besonderer Beliebtheit. Mit Untergangsprognosen lässt sich allemal mehr – auch mediale – Aufmerksamkeit erzielen, als mit differenzierteren Analysen und auch positiven Nachrichten, dass viel an Bewusstsein geschaffen worden ist, dem auch an allen Ecken und Enden der Welt Millionen von Taten folgen. Nicht nur als Vater zweier Töchter, sondern auch als nunmehr beinahe schon 30 Jahre an unterschiedlichen Universitäten Lehrender, empfinde ich es geradezu skandalös, dass jungen Menschen systematisch eingetrichtert wird, sie lebten in der schlechtesten aller denkbaren Welten, die ohnedies bald dem Untergang geweiht ist. Der Romantisierung des globalen Unheils – als neuer kultur- und zivilisationskritischer Narrativ – kann ich nichts abgewinnen. Natürlich sehen sich die Menschen gewaltigen Problemen und Herausforderungen gegenüberstehen und natürlich ist es fraglich – siehe den Anfang dieses Beitrags – ob trotz all der Bemühungen die Zeit für adäquate Lösungen nicht zu knapp wird. Aber misst man Fortschritt nicht nur an Problemen sondern auch an den realen Lebensverhältnissen der auf diesem Planeten lebenden Menschen, so hat es noch keine Epoche in der Geschichte der Menschheit gegeben, in der die Menschen – bei noch vor kurzer Zeit unvorstellbar langer Lebenserwartung – derart gut, relativ abgesichert und auch relativ schmerzlos gelebt haben!

„Warum sieht das denn keiner?", fragt der Physiker und Kulturphilosoph Johannes Schmidl, der zwei ausgezeichnete Bücher über Utopien und Dystopien bezüglich des Umgangs mit natürlichen Ressourcen geschrieben hat. In einem von ihm verfassten Artikel heißt es:

> *„Lebten 1900 noch 85 Prozent der Weltbevölkerung in extremer Armut, sind es 2015 rund 10 Prozent. Die Armut verschwindet mit großer Geschwindigkeit, die ärmsten Länder wachsen am schnellsten; die Lebenserwartung steigt weltweit, allein in Afrika hat sie sich seit Mitte des 20. Jahrhunderts auf über 60 Jahre verdoppelt. Starb um 1800 noch die Hälfte der Kinder vor dem fünften Lebensjahr, sind es heute weniger als 4 %. Und damit nimmt die Wachstumsrate der Menschheit dramatisch ab: von 2,1 % pro Jahr Mitte der 60er Jahre auf heute etwa die Hälfte dessen. Warum sehen wir das nicht? Warum lassen sich diese Geschichten nicht erzählen? Wir haben in Europa vieles aus den kühnsten Erzählungen der Utopien verwirklicht. Der Rest der Welt holt jetzt aber deutlich auf, die vormals Unterprivilegierten steigen in unseren vormaligen Adelsstand auf – und damit werden wir alle allmählich zu wohlsituierten Erden- oder Weltbürgern. Europa geht nicht unter, sondern, wenn man so will: es triumphiert durch die Früchte seiner globalisierten Aufklärung weltweit. Prinzipien und Methoden der Rationalität und die wesentlich auf deren Basis entwickelten Technologien setzen sich durch – im Widerstand gegen die eingesessenen Macht-, Clan-, und Stammeskulturen und die etablierten machtbewussten Religionen."*[22]

Sozialökologische Transformationen und Öffentlichkeitsarbeit

Unsere Abteilung „Bildung und Forschung für internationale Entwicklungszusammenarbeit" in der OeAD-GmbH ist im Wesentlichen in drei Arbeitsbereichen tätig. Sowohl in der „Kommission für Entwicklungsforschung" (KEF) als auch in dem „Austrian Partnership Programme in Higher Education and Research for Development" (APPEAR)[23], das von der Österreichischen Entwicklungszusammenarbeit finanziert wird, geht es um:

- die Förderung, Anbahnung und Organisation von partizipativen Partnerschaften in Forschung und Lehre zwischen österreichischen Hochschulen/wissenschaftlichen Institutionen und Universitäten/wissenschaftlichen Institutionen in Less und Least Developed Countries im Bereich der Entwicklungsforschung,

- die Sichtbarmachung der Entwicklungsforschung als breites transdisziplinäres Forschungsfeld, das ergebnisorientiert und zielgruppenspezifisch die Lebensbedingungen der Menschen in den Partnerländern verbessert und die Kapazitätenentwicklung in Wissenschaft und Forschung fördert, und um

- Öffentlichkeitsarbeit und Vernetzungsaktivitäten in Österreich, die zu einer breiteren Akzeptanz der Entwicklungsforschung als wichtiger Beitrag zur Verwirklichung der Sustainable Development Goals (SDGs) führen.

Durch unsere Wissenschaftskooperationen und Aktivitäten in der Öffentlichkeitsarbeit sind wir tagtäglich bemüht, eine kritische, transdisziplinäre Entwicklungsforschung in den Dienst der notwendigen Transformationen und damit in den Dienst der Zukunftsfähigkeit unserer Welt zu stellen. Neben der Projektarbeit in Forschung und Lehre und auch der studentischen Mobilität, die wir im Rahmen von APPEAR organisieren,[24] scheint uns auch insbesondere die Öffentlichkeitsarbeit wichtig, um das Verständnis der Notwendigkeit von Veränderungen im Sinne der hier referierten Themen zu fördern.

Auch die Öffentlichkeitsarbeit der KEF richtet sich einerseits an spezifisch wissenschaftliche, aber andererseits auch an breiter gefasste Zielgruppen. Der Scientific Community – die KEF sieht sich hier als Plattform der Information und der Kommunikation – werden Diskussionsveranstaltungen, Projektpräsentationen, Fact Sheets, die Unterstützung von Open Access-Publikationen, Round Table Gespräche etc. angeboten. Zudem vernetzen wir Akteure und Akteurinnen des Forschungsfeldes, sei es nun aufgrund ähnlicher wissenschaftlicher Fragestellungen oder aufgrund regionaler Expertise, und bilden einen Transmissionsriemen für den Austausch zwischen Wissenschaft, NGOs, inter- und transnationalen Organisationen und zuweilen auch der Wirtschaft. Neben der Projektdatenbank und der Archivierung eigener und aus KEF-Projekten resultierender Publikationen, stellt unsere Webseite auch ein News-Service dar, das interessierte User auf wichtige Veranstaltungen, Konferenzen, Ausschreibungen, aber auch inhaltliche Entwicklungen und Diskurse dieses Forschungsfeldes aktuell aufmerksam macht.

Die Öffentlichkeitsarbeit für eine breitere, sowohl an generellen wissenschaftlichen Fragen als auch speziellen entwicklungspolitischen Diskursen interessierte Zielgruppe, gestaltet das KEF-Team auf Basis langjähriger Expertise in multimedialer Darstellung von Forschungs- und Diskussionsinhalten. Zentrales Medium ist die ORF Ö1 Campus Radiosendung „Welt im Ohr", die zwei bis dreimal im Monat, jeweils an den Freitagen der ungeraden Wochen, vorwiegend einstündige Live-Diskussionen, aber auch vorproduzierte Sendungen rund um die Themen der KEF- und APPEAR-Projekte, der Diskurse in den Bereichen Entwicklungsforschung und Entwicklungszusammenarbeit und der SDGs, bzw. der aus ihnen resultierenden gesellschaftspolitischen Fragestellungen und Lösungsvorschläge, sendet. Alle Sendungen sind als Podcast abrufbar und werden auch auf den unterschiedlichsten Plattformen unserer Medienpartner verbreitet. 2017 wurden fünf Jahre „Welt im Ohr" im Rahmen einer Live-Veranstaltung im ORF-RadioCafe im Funkhaus Wien gefeiert und auch eine Jubiläums-CD „Fünf Jahre Welt im Ohr" präsentiert.

Auch andere Kooperationen mit dem Sender ORF-Ö1 haben vielfach die Projekte, Forschungsbemühungen und Ergebnisse der KEF-Projekte in unterschiedlichen Sendungsleisten – z. B. „Dimensionen – Welt der Wissenschaft", Radiokolleg, „Von Tag zu Tag" etc. – dargestellt. Zudem werden die Aktivitäten der KEF regelmäßig in Print-Medien, auf Online-Plattformen, über Facebook, Twitter und auch in den „hauseigenen" OeAD-News präsentiert. Neben dieser medialen Schiene sind der KEF Veranstaltungen wichtig, die sich nicht nur an einen sehr speziellen Kreis von Wissenschaftler/innen richten, sondern auch an ein breiteres Publikum. So werden seit Jahren von der KEF Filmtage organisiert – zuletzt auch in Kooperation mit großen Festivals wie „this human world – das Internationale Filmfestival der Menschenrechte", die einem cineastischen Publikum Einblick in die Strukturen und die Relevanz der Entwicklungsforschung bieten. Bei diesen Abenden wird immer ein themenrelevanter Film gespielt und hernach dessen Inhalt im Lichte von KEF-Forschungsprojekten von Projektmitarbeiter/innen aus dem Inland und den jeweiligen Partnerländern kontextualisiert. Seit 2016 ist die KEF auch eine Kooperation mit dem Naturhistorischen Museum in Wien eingegangen. An diesen Abenden werden KEF-Projekte einem interessierten Publikum in deutscher Sprache vorgestellt, wobei den Fragen und der Diskussion des Publikums ein breiter Raum eingeräumt wird.

Öffentlich finanzierte Forschung hat eine Bringschuld bezüglich der Darstellung der durch sie generierten Ergebnisse – insbesondere dann, wenn es sich nicht um manchmal schwer verständliche Grundlagenforschung, sondern um Themen handelt, die Menschen – hier oder woanders – ganz direkt betreffen. Entwicklungsforschung richtet sich an konkrete Menschen und „Stakeholder" – wie es in der derzeitigen Terminologie heißt –, ist lösungsorientiert und will zum systematischen Verständnis von komplexen sozialen, ökonomischen, ökologischen und immer wieder auch politischen Verhältnissen beitragen. Zudem impliziert Entwicklungsforschung einen normativen Aspekt, denn es geht nicht um ein wertneutrales Generieren von wissenschaftlichen Ergebnissen, sondern um deren gezielte Nutzung für die Verbesserung von konkreten Lebensbedingungen. Dieser normative Ansatz deckt sich mit den normativen Zielen der SDGs, die von der Staatengemeinschaft beschlossen wurden, um den Menschen unterschiedlichster Staaten und Kulturen eine Vision und ein Programm zur Umsetzung einer nachhaltigen Organisation von Leben auf unserem Planeten zur Hand zu geben. All diese Aspekte sind Grund genug, um die Öffentlichkeitsarbeit der KEF weit über die Sphäre der Scientific Community hinauswachsen zu lassen und vor allem auch jene Menschen zu erreichen, die bislang nur peripher von Entwicklungsforschung und Entwicklungszusammenarbeit berührt worden sind.

Zu den Arbeiten des Nachwuchspreises für Entwicklungsforschung 2015 und 2017

Der „Österreichische Preis für Entwicklungsforschung" ist nicht nur, aber auch eine Maßnahme der KEF-Öffentlichkeitsarbeit, die wir dem ehemaligen Wissenschaftsminister Em. o. Univ.-Prof. Mag. Dr. Karlheinz Töchterle zu verdanken haben, der diese Auszeichnung im Jahr 2013 institutionalisiert hat. Einerseits geht es um die Ehrung wichtiger Leistungen für das Forschungsfeld, andererseits auch um deren Wahrnehmung innerhalb und außerhalb der Scientific Community. Der von einer qualifizierten Fachjury entschiedene Preis kann als weiteres Zeichen dafür gesehen werden, dass lösungsorientierten Ansätzen im Bereich nachhaltiger Entwicklung und im Kontext entwicklungspolitischer Interventionen jedenfalls eine wichtige Rolle zukommt, die sichtbar gemacht und eben auch feierlich gewürdigt werden soll.

Die in diesem Reader versammelten Texte stellen eine Auswahl der Einreichungen der Jahre 2015 und 2017 dar. Ihnen allen ist gemeinsam, dass sie wichtige wissenschaftliche und auch forschungspragmatische Aspekte behandeln, die als exemplarisch für dieses Forschungsfeld gelten können. In dem Beitrag von Gerhard Adam mit dem Titel „Sustainable Tourism and Development in Bhutan" wird der sanfte und zahlenmäßig bewusst begrenzte Kulturtourismus im Himalaya-Königreich als Teil des „Gross National Happiness"-Konzeptes kritisch analysiert, wobei auf die Potentiale gleichermaßen eingegangen wird, wie auf mögliche, durch Tourismus entstehende Defizite. Erstaunlich an der bhutanischen Tourismusstrategie freilich ist die Betonung der Balance zwischen Gast, Gastgeber und der natürlichen Umwelt – ein durchaus als holistisch zu bezeichnendes Konzept, welches das „Well-Being" aller Akteure und Stakeholder und auch die Schonung der natürlichen Ressourcen in den Mittelpunkt rückt. Mit diesem Zugang ist auch die kulturelle Identität der Gastgeber angesprochen, die in Bhutan als besonders schützenswert erachtet wird. Obzwar vom Tourismus in Bhutan die wirklich Armen im Lande kaum profitieren – wie das zumeist der Fall ist –, leistet er einen wichtigen Beitrag zur Reduzierung ökonomischer Abhängigkeit, wie etwa die vom Nachbarland Indien.

Der Siegertext des Nachwuchspreises 2017 stammt von der Kultur- und Sozialanthropologin Salomé Ritterband, die ihren Master im gleichen Jahr an der Universität Wien abgeschlossen hat. Ihr Beitrag basiert auf ihrer Masterarbeit und titelt „Tradition Re-Interpreted – A New Generation. The Children of the Ju/'hoansi San Rehearsing Traditional Heritage in the Context of Cultural Tourism in the Tsumkwe District of Namibia". Ausgehend von einer Feldforschung im Norden Namibias werden die zentralen Aspekte des Living Museum-Konzeptes kritisch reflektiert. Der methodische Zugang dabei ist außergewöhnlich und ethnographisch originell – es sind die Kinder des Dorfes, die zur primären Erhebungsquelle werden, durch deren Erzählungen und Spiele dem Narrativ nachgespürt wird, der hier Kultur einerseits an Touristen vermittelt, andererseits aber auch als Identitätsstifter für die San-Bevölkerung revitalisiert wird. In der Lebenswelt der Kinder wird die „playing culture", also die im doppelten Wortsinn gespielte und vorgespielte Kultur, zu einer zweiten Identität, die sinnstiftend und positiv wahrgenommen wird. Zudem lassen sich daraus für die Erwachsenen des Dorfes auch neue Einkommen generieren und das soziale und kulturelle Selbstbewusstsein gegenüber Außen wird gestärkt. Die Studie und der Text von Frau Ritterband zeigen, dass „Folklorisierung" nicht unbedingt zu Identitätsdiffusion und Kulturverlust führen muss, sondern innerhalb bestimmter Kontexte zu „Empowerment" und spürbarer ökonomischer Besserstellung beitragen kann. Nachhaltiger Tourismus für Entwicklung scheint in diesem, teils von den Betroffenen enthusiastisch gelebten Konzept jedenfalls eingelöst zu sein.

Der Arbeit von Maria Katelieva mit dem Titel „Social and cultural impacts of tourism: The Case of the Bulgarian Villages Gorno Draglishte and Dobarsko" geht auf die beginnende Tourismusentwicklung in zwei bulgarischen Dörfern ein. Im Rahmen einer vierwöchigen Feldforschung wurden die positiven und möglichen negativen Auswirkungen des nachhaltigen Tourismus untersucht, wobei positiv und negativ mitunter auch theoretisch nicht so leicht voneinander zu trennen sind. Der analytische Blick der Autorin richtet sich insbesondere auf die Rollenverteilung und auf das Rollenverständnis der handelnden Akteure, die allesamt eine positive Identifizierung mit ihrer „traditionellen Kultur" aufweisen. Dies zeigt sich von der Bedeutung der Alltagskleidung über die Kulinarik bis hin zur Musik und dem Tanz auf vielfältige Weise. Entlang einiger theoretischer Ansätze zeichnet die Autorin ein sozialwissenschaftlich dichtes Bild der Funktion und der Bedeutung des durch den Tourismus neu entstandenen Kulturbewusstseins. Kultur ist etwas, auf das die Bevölkerung in diesem Kontext stolz sein kann und was die Vergangenheit mit der Zukunft – auch mit neuen ökonomischen Möglichkeiten – verbindet. So werden diese Kulturaktivitäten auch für bulgarische Medien interessant, ebenso wie für englische Touristen die meinen, hier wäre es so wie vor 60 Jahren in ihren Herkunftsgebieten. Auch wenn Authentizität gleichermaßen wie deren Gegenteil eine soziale Konstruktion sein mag, so bleibt doch die Frage, ob in „Privates" interveniert werden darf. Für die Autorin hängt die Beantwortung dieser Frage an der Dichte des nachhaltigen Tourismus. Solange für die Bewohner/innen des Dorfes noch Zeit bleibt ihren eigenen Aktivitäten, Festen und rituellen Zyklen (z. B. Ostern, Weihnachten) nachzugehen und sie nicht ständig das „Geschäft mit den Touristen" bedienen müssen, solange sieht die Autorin keine kulturellen Schäden entstehen. Im Gegenteil – der nachhaltige Tourismus erfüllt eine wichtige Funktion, denn so wird eine Kultur dargeboten, die ohne diese Aktivitäten einfach verschwunden wäre.

Im dritten Teil des vorliegenden Buches werden Kurzfassungen von wissenschaftlichen Arbeiten vorgestellt, die zum Nachwuchspreis 2015 unter dem Motto „Städte im Wandel. Entwicklung und Nachhaltigkeit der Städte im globalen Süden" eingereicht wurden. Johannes Knierzinger erforscht in seinem Beitrag „Unternehmerische Kontrolle in guineischen Bauxitstädten: Wie man von einem Löwen springt" Bauxit-Städte in Guinea, wobei ihn insbesondere die herrschaftssoziologisch bedeutsame Frage interesssiert, wie extreme Abhängigkeiten der dort lebenden Menschen von hierarchischen Metastrukturen vermieden oder abgefedert werden können. Der Siegertext des Nachwuchspreises 2015 wurde von

Robert Hafner verfasst und titelt „handlung | macht | raum: Urbane Material-sammler-Kooperativen und ihre Livelihoods-Strategien in Buenos Aires". Auf Basis bereits bestehender Forschungsarbeiten in Städten wie Kairo, São Paulo oder Delhi entwickelt er seine Studie in Buenos Aires anhand des historischen Über-gangs vom informellen Müllsammeln zu institutionalisierten Formen der auch politisch bedeutsam werdenden Materialsammler-Kooperativen. Auch auf die sich daraus ergebenden Konflikte und neuen Machtkonstellationen wird detail-reich eingegangen.

Verunmöglicht Armut umweltgerechtes Handeln? fragt sich die Kultur- und Sozialanthropologin Elisabeth Huber in ihrem Beitrag „Über das Potential der ‚Armen' in westafrikanischen Städten, umweltgerecht zu handeln". Sie hat umfang-reiche quantitative Studien ebenso ausgewertet, wie teilnehmende Beobachtungen durchgeführt, auch in Mali und Burkina Faso ergänzende Forschungen zu dem Thema betrieben. Nach wie vor ist es für in Armut lebende Menschen de facto unmöglich ein relevantes Umweltbewusstsein zu entwickeln, was zu einer per-manenten Verschmutzung des öffentlichen Raumes und auch zu Ressourcenver-schwendung führt. Die Autorin unterbreitet in ihrer als Dissertation approbierten Arbeit aber auch Lösungsvorschläge wie die aktuelle Situation verbessert werden kann. Die ebenfalls als Dissertation konzipierte Arbeit von Lorenz Probst titelt: „Drivers and constraints of an innovation towards improved vegetable safety in urban West Africa (Benin, Ghana and Burkina Faso)". In ihr wird dem Zusam-menhang zwischen Urbanisierung und Veränderung der Ernährungsgewohnhei-ten in Hinblick auf soziale Innovation im Bereich des Gemüseanbaus nachgegan-gen. Faktoren werden identifiziert, die nachhaltige Anbaumethoden fördern oder hemmen, die eine Zertifizierung ökologischer Landwirtschaft und deren Vermark-tung ermöglichen und die Lernprozesse entlang der gesamten Wertschöpfungskette begünstigen.

Entwicklungsforschung als transdisziplinärer Forschungsbereich ist zu einem wichtigen Instrument in der wissenschaftlichen Begleitung der Realisierung der Nachhaltigen Entwicklungsziele (SDGs) geworden. Nicht nur die Indikatoren zur Messung dieser Fortschritte, sondern auch die einzelnen Schritte, die zu den jewei-ligen Etappenzielen führen, werden durch Wissenschaft und Forschung maßgeblich bestimmt. Die Ziele der sozialökologischen Transformation konnten nur auf Basis evidenzbasierter Empirie entwickelt werden, die Implementierung der SDGs wird auch weitgehend von der Kompetenz eines Wissenschafts- und Forschungsbereiches abhängen, der sich auf die Praxis des sozialen Zusammenlebens und auf die Lösung der dringlichsten globalen Herausforderungen bezieht. Alle Themen der Beiträge dieses Buches haben in der einen oder anderen Weise auch mit jener sozial-ökologischen Transformation zu tun, die Voraussetzung für die Eliminierung der extremen Armut und auch Voraussetzung zur Erlangung ökonomischer, kulturel-ler und ökologischer Nachhaltigkeit ist. Der Erreichung dieser Ziele wird sich die Kommission für Entwicklungsforschung (KEF) weiterhin verpflichtet fühlen und sie mit allen Mitteln fördern und begleiten.

Anmerkungen

1 Zum Österreichischen Preis für Entwicklungsforschung siehe: https://kef-research.at/de/kommunikation/entwicklungsforschungspreis.

2 Vgl. dazu die Website der Vereinten Nationen: http://www.tourism4development2017.org.

3 Dieses transdisziplinäre Forschungsfeld ist in folgender Untersuchung analysiert, strukturiert und auch nach disziplinären Überschneidungen dargestellt worden: Witjes, Nina/Novy, Andreas/Schlögl, Matthias/Obrecht, Andreas J. (2012): *Wissensallianzen für Entwicklung. EntwicklungsForschungsNetzwerk(EnFoNet) – Strukturen, Akteure & Netzwerke der österreichischen Entwicklungsforschung.* Herausgegeben von der Österreichischen Forschungsstiftung für Internationale Entwicklung (ÖFSE Edition Band 18). Wien: Südwind Verlag.

4 Siehe dazu das Mission Statement der Kommission für Entwicklungsforschung (KEF): https://kef-research.at/de/ueber-uns/organisation-und-ziele.

5 Ein Überblick über laufende und abgeschlossene Projekte findet sich auf: https://kef-research.at/de/projekte/laufende-projekte.

6 Die Liste der Entwicklungsländer, die vom Development Assistance Committe der OECD als Empfängerländer staatlicher Entwicklungsgelder definiert sind und die auch für die KEF förderungsrelevant sind findet sich unter: http://www.oecd.org/dac/stats/daclist.htm.

7 Alle KEF-Projekte und Ergebnisse liegen in digitalisierter Form in der KEF-Projektdatenbank vor: https://kef-research.at/de/projekte/projektdatenbank.

8 Bei Redaktionsschluss dieses Buches war der österreichische ODA-Prozentsatz am Bruttonationalprodukt für das Jahr 2017 noch nicht offiziell bekannt gegeben. Demgemäß handelt es sich bei dem angeführten Prozentsatz um Prognosedaten. Laut ODA-Vorausmeldung an den Entwicklungshilfeausschuss der OECD beträgt die vorläufige ODA 2017 1,09 Milliarden Euro bzw. 0,30 % des BNP.

9 Zitat in allen drei synoptischen Evangelien fast gleichlautend: „Nochmals sage ich euch: Eher geht ein Kamel durch ein Nadelöhr, als dass ein Reicher in das Reich Gottes gelangt." – Matthäus 19,24.

10 Vgl. dazu Andreas J. Obrecht in der Zeitschrift *Der Standard*, Kommentar der Anderen: *Globale Armut: Es gibt Hoffnung. Eine kritische Replik zu Philipp Blom* vom 29.12.2017: https://derstandard.at/2000071211031/Globale-Armut-Es-gibt-Hoffnung [18.06.2018].

11 Inflations- und kaufkraftbereinigt nach dem Indikator der Weltbank weniger als 1,90 US-Dollar pro Person und Tag.

12 http://www.worldbank.org/en/topic/poverty [27.12.2017].

13 United Nations Population Devision: https://esa.un.org/unpd/wpp.

14 Bewusst wird hier nicht auf regionale Ungleichzeitigkeiten bei der Entwicklung der Wachstumsraten eingegangen. Insbesondere einzelne afrikanische Länder – z. B. Nigeria – werden noch länger hohe Wachstumsraten verzeichnen, was den hier skizzierten globalen Trend freilich nicht umkehrt.

15 Siehe hierzu: https://ourworldindata.org/life-expectancy sowie http://www.who.int/gho/mortality_burden_disease/life_tables/en.

16 Vgl. dazu meine Replik auf ein Interview mit dem Kulturphilosophen Philipp Blom (https://derstandard.at/2000068468821/Philipp-BlomDie-Erde-braucht-uns-nicht-Zur-Person) in der Zeitschrift *Der Standard*. So wie viele Intellektuelle beschwört auch Blom immer wieder ein düsteres und kulturpessimistisches Bild der Zukunft, was in vielen Aspekten durchaus richtig sein mag, in anderen freilich weit über das Ziel hinausschießt und vor allem empirische Befunde außer Acht lässt. Dass Armut nicht reduziert werden konnte und die heutige Gesellschaft diesbezüglich keine sie tragende Hoffnung mehr hat, entbehrt jeder Evidenz: https://derstandard.at/2000071211031/Globale-Armut-Es-gibt-Hoffnung [18.06.2018].

17 Zu unterschiedlichen Wissensformen und -konzepten im interkulturellen Vergleich siehe: Obrecht, Andreas J. (2014): *Wozu wissen wollen? Wissen – Herrschaft – Welterfahrung. Ein Beitrag zur Wissensdiskussion aus kultur- und wissenssoziologischer Perspektive.* Wien/Ohlsdorf: Edition Ausblick.

18 Zur 7. Österreichischen Entwicklungstagung auf der Website des Paulo Freire Zentrums unter www. entwicklungstagung.at .

19 Diese Veranstaltung fand am 17. November 2017 statt. Den Hauptpreis erhielten ex aequo die „Österreichische Forschungsstiftung für Internationale Entwicklung" (ÖFSE) und der Verein „Frauen*solidarität" für besondere Leistungen im Bereich der Entwicklungsforschung, den Nach-

wuchspreis erhielt die Kultur- und Sozialanthropologin Salomé Ritterband (siehe ihren Beitrag in diesem Buch). Für die ÖFSE nahm den Preis Direktor Werner Raza entgegen, für die „Frauensolidarität" die langjährige Obfrau Ulrike Lunacek. Eine einstündige Radiosendung mit den Preisträger/innen findet sich unter dem Titel „„Die Zukunft die wir haben wollen': Sternstunden der Österreichischen Entwicklungsforschung" unter https://kef-research.at/de/aktuelles/artikel/2017/12/die-zukunft-die-wir-haben-wollen-sternstunden-der-oesterreichischen-entwicklungsforschung/.

20 Vgl. dazu etwa den Artikel des Tourismusforschers Friedl, Harald A. (2017*): Nachhaltiger Tourismus für Entwicklung. Um wen oder was geht es hier tatsächlich?* In: Tourismus Wissen – quarterly. 8/2017.

21 Teile dieser Fragenbeantwortung wurden unter dem Titel „Kein Kapitalismus ist auch keine Lösung" auf der Tagungswebseite veröffentlicht: https://www.pfz.at/article1992.htm. Der Titel ist einem ausgezeichneten Buch von Ulrike Hermann entlehnt, die darin die Krise der heutigen Ökonomie mit Smith, Marx und Keynes abhandelt (2016, Westend Verlag), auch wenn die nachfolgenden Darstellungen mit diesem lesenswerten Buch nur bedingt zu tun haben.

22 Johannes Schmidl: *Literarische Utopien: Sind wir reif für die Insel?* In der Zeitschrift *Der Standard*, Kommentar der Anderen vom 05.08.2017: https://derstandard.at/2000062277995/Sind-wir-reif-fuer-die-Insel [18.06.2018]. Vgl. dazu auch: Schmidl, Johannes (2016): Bauplan für eine Insel – 500 Jahre Utopia. Wien: Sonderzahl Verlag.

23 Siehe hierzu: www.kef-research.at und www.appear.at

24 Insgesamt konnten im Rahmen von APPEAR rund 70 Studierende aus afrikanischen, lateinamerikanischen und asiatischen Ländern ein Master- bzw. PhD-Programm an österreichischen Universitäten beginnen. Mehr als zwei Drittel von ihnen haben bereits erfolgreich abgeschlossen, der Rest wird bis zum Ende der jetzigen Programmphase im November 2020 die Studien ebenfalls beenden.

II Nachhaltiger Tourismus für Entwicklung –

Texte des Österreichischen Nachwuchspreises für Entwicklungsforschung 2017

Gerhard Adam

Sustainable Tourism and Development in Bhutan

Introduction

The profile of tourism in Bhutan shows evident spatial, temporal and social disparity. This is not only a key finding which has to be anticipated beforehand, it also sums up in one sentence the problem of this paper and that of the Bhutanese tourism industry. The resulting purpose of this work is to support the key stakeholders of the Bhutanese tourism system to rebalance the tourism sector by developing new tourism products. In order to succeed, these products have to be in line with the development goals of Bhutan and ought to address the socioeconomic challenges of this small kingdom sandwiched between the two most populated countries in the world.

This paper focuses on an adaptive paradigm shaped by sustainable, community-based and pro-poor tourism. As it focuses exclusively on Bhutan, it provides neither a general overview of tourism worldwide and in developing countries, nor does it take part in the crucial discussion about the efficiency of sustainability measures in mass tourism vs. alternative tourism.

The current paper constitutes an updated extract of the author's Master's thesis entitled *Sustainable Pro-Poor Tourism in Bhutan*, which further comprises a case study carried out in the Phobjikha Valley in Western Bhutan.[1] At the time of submission in December 2014, this was the first comprehensive academic analysis of tourism and its interrelation to development in Bhutan since Tandi Dorji's article *Sustainability of Tourism in Bhutan* published in 2001.

Sustainable Tourism in Theory

Tourism as a field of research is inherently inter- and multidisciplinary.[2] Any comprehensive theoretical and practical research in tourism must therefore follow a holistic approach. This is not only true for the field of tourism as a whole but also for its diverse subfields, in particular for sustainable tourism. Weaver[3] discusses this holistic approach in the context of the broader concept of sustainable development. The essence of his remarks – inspired by systems science – also applies to sustainable tourism, not least because this paradigm is derived from the concept of sustainable development. On a global scale, each and every human activity, whether touristic or not, is limited by the closed system called the *world*. Therefore, as Butler states correctly, "we cannot hope to achieve sustainability in one sector alone, when each is linked to and dependent upon the others"[4].

Cater and Lowman provide one of the innumerable listings of key findings, which are the outcome of a broad academic discussion over recent decades: According to the understanding of these authors, a holistic approach in sustainable tourism takes into consideration nature, society and economics in equal parts. The cooperation and interaction of all stakeholders is guaranteed by a bottom-up process which spatially passes from the local and national level to the global level. Public-private partnership (PPP) is the focal point of a holistic approach in tourism while at the same time the interests of future stakeholders are considered in the spirit of the *Brundtland Report*[5]. Other authors, like Zimmermann[6], who introduces culture as a fourth level, or Briassoulis[7], who extends the scope to the principle of subsidiarity, add or omit certain patterns.

The holistic approach as portrayed above serves as a theoretical framework for this paper. It is not the purpose of this work to fully elaborate on the development of the different subfields of tourism, which is mapped in the "extensive literature that exists on sustainable tourism"[8]. This chapter rather provides a brief theoretical overview that emphasises certain paradigms, namely the three approaches applied in this paper: sustainable tourism, community-based tourism and pro-poor tourism. A closer analysis of the academic debate on sustainability in tourism is detailed inter alia in Hall/Lew[9], Weaver[10] and in the four volume publication *Sustainable Tourism* edited by Page/Connell[11].

Each of these three paradigms accentuates a certain component of the relationship between visitors, local community and environment, while their belonging to the category alternative tourism is their common denominator. Alternative tourism – Mowforth and Munt use the umbrella term "new tourism"[12], whereas Wheeller uses "responsible tourism"[13] – is understood as a "deliberate alternative"[14] to unsustainable mass tourism. In the lengthy academic debate there is as yet no clear agreement, neither about its definition nor about its conceptual and practical boundaries. In opposition to mass tourism, though, it is an undisputed fact that all its sub-categories take account of the environmental, economic and socio-cultural impacts of tourism.[15] As early as 1981, Dernoi provided a five-point list of characteristics which essentially emphasised the polarisation between alternative and mass tourism, e.g. small vs. large scale, locally vs. externally oriented or low vs. high impact. In fact, as Dernoi rightly concludes, these dichotomous ideal types are "rarely encountered in their purest form because of the sheer complexity [of tourism]".[16] Almost every alternative activity in tourism depends on some kind of interaction with the conventional tourism industry. Amongst many other authors Weaver points out the classic example of falling back upon the service of international airlines, which illustrates most clearly this dependency or "link" as denominated by Weaver.[17]

Sustainable tourism, community-based tourism and pro-poor tourism are just three of the "seemingly endless list of new tourism terms"[18]. Mowforth/Munt list five of these paradigms as the "front runners"[19]. Aside from the aforementioned paradigms, ecotourism as the "conscience of sustainable tourism"[20] and fair trade tourism are the flagships of alternative tourism. This chapter, however, discusses only those aspects which are of significance to the development of the tourism industry of Bhutan. A comprehensive overview of the history and typology of alternative tourism products and its potential problems can be found in Weaver[21].

Sustainable Tourism

At the very beginning, it has to be stressed that there is still no universally accepted definition of sustainable tourism. Regardless of a long-standing academic and political debate, sustainable tourism remains a "nebulous concept"[22]. To outline its characteristics, authors like Hall/Lew[23], Hardy et al.[24] and Page/Connell[25] quote the historical evolution's milestones of the concept of sustainability, like *The Brandt Report*, the *World Conversation Strategy* and the so-called *Brundtland Report*, which were equally influential to the paradigms of sustainable development and sustainable tourism. Additionally Weaver (2006) portrays the development of the last decade by focusing in particular on ecotourism whose success story culminated in the declaration of 2002 as International Year of Ecotourism[26].

In 2004, the Committee on Sustainable Development of Tourism of the World Tourism Organisation of the United Nations did attempt to address the "vast range of definitions"[27] as well as to revise the one published by UNWTO itself in 1995. Since the early 1980s UNWTO has taken the leading role in the formulation and diffusion of sustainable tourism policies and practices.[28] The outcome of the 2004 UNWTO-revision must be seen less as a definition of sustainable tourism than as a set of principles for a sustainable development of tourism. The then "conceptual definition" emphasises the establishment of a suitable balance between the environmental, social and economic aspects of tourism guaranteeing its long-term sustainability[29]. Based on the balance between these three dimensions, UNWTO highlights that sustainable tourism should

> "make optimal use of environmental resources [...], respect the socio-cultural authenticity of host communities [and] provid[e] socio-economic benefits to all stakeholders". Furthermore, sustainable tourism "requires the informed participation of all relevant stakeholders, as well as strong political leadership [and] is a continuous process [that] requires constant monitoring of impacts [to] maintain [a] high level of tourist satisfaction".[30]

Page/Connell indicates that, apart from formulating "official" principles, the approach of UNWTO confirms once again the main remit of sustainable tourism: striking a suitable balance between the host, the guest and the environment to maximise the benefits and minimise the costs.[31] Unlike in the early years of the academic discussion about sustainable tourism, today it is a matter of course that this does not imply the prevention of growth but the "frequently quoted and already much-abused development strategy of 'qualitative growth'"[32].

All the aforementioned aspects are incorporated in the famous concept of the "magic pentagon of sustainable tourism". Müller founds his magic pentagon on the following five cornerstones: (1) economic health; (2) subjective well-being of the locals; (3) unspoilt nature and protection of resources; (4) healthy culture; and (5) optimum satisfaction of guest requirements[33].[34] The basic idea of this graphical representation is to illustrate that none of the cornerstones is predominant, not even the economic one. In view of the present situation, as Müller admits, "this concept represents an upgrading of social and environmental interests and a comparative downgrading of purely economic ones"[35].

The five cornerstones of the magic pentagon might be seen as an application of the theoretical concept of the "sustainable trinity" on tourism. By focusing on economic, social and ecological sustainability, in practice financing of a tourism product is often not taken into account. In the opinion of the author of this paper, financing, namely financial sustainability, should therefore be introduced as a fourth dimension. Financial sustainability does not exactly equate to economic sustainability. On the temporal scale of the development of a tourism product, financial sustainability refers rather to the phases of identification, consultation, planning and implementation, whereas economic sustainability refers to the phases of operation, management, monitoring and evaluation. Consequently, financial sustainability guarantees the initial financing of a tourism product, whereas economic sustainability guarantees the generation of net benefits. However, in theory as well as in practice, this semantic distinction is not or only rarely considered. Nevertheless, financial sustainability is no less than the basic condition for the success of any tourism product aspiring to attain the "sustainable trinity". Since the initial financing of a tourism product has to be addressed first, the imperative of financial sustainability needs to be qualified as the foundation of the five cornerstones of the magic pentagon.

By focusing on the suitable balance of the "sustainable trinity", many authors not only forget about the importance of the financial sustainability but also about the need to differentiate between social and cultural sustainability. In short, a community as a whole might be able to absorb external inputs and to continue functioning in social harmony. However, within the community, these external inputs, whether they are perceived as positive or negative, might initiate cultural change. Mowforth/Munt point to the interrelation of society and culture by stating that "[e]ven if the society survives its culture may be irreversibly altered"[36]. The paradigm of community-based tourism which is detailed in the following has a lot of common ground with sustainable tourism, but places more attention on these social and cultural aspects, in particular community participation.

Community-based Tourism

Community-based tourism has become synonymous with an actively participating local community. Though, so far few authors have paid much attention to defining community.[37] Hall/Lew follow a fairly sociological approach stressing spatial proximity as essential to the formation of community,[38] whereas Weaver firstly puts his focus on distinguishing newcomers and long-time residents[39]. By also taking into account non-resident property holders, seasonal occupants of second homes and members of indigenous communities, Weaver equates community with rootedness in place.[40] This is particularly true for indigenous communities who have never been residents but who have a strong familial and cultural attachment to their community lands. In the opinion of the author of this paper it is most suitable to concretise Weaver's concept of rootedness in place: Rather than the objective evaluation of rootedness by spatiotemporal indicators, it is the subjective sense of attachment and devotion to a certain community which is decisive. This concept of subjective rootedness also takes into consideration newcomers who quickly develop a strong sense of belonging to the local community.

Community-based tourism replenishes the dimensions of sustainable tourism – environmental, social, economic as well as financial and cultural sustainability – with the dimension of political sustainability, which enables the participation of the local community. To that effect, in this paper political sustainability equates to participation.

To what degree a local community participates varies widely depending on the nature of the different projects. In tourism, Zimmermann defines participation as a two-way communication process between the government, the private sector and the public[41]. The unequal distribution of power between the local community and other stakeholders is reflected in the widely accepted typology of participation by Pretty, detailed, inter alia, in Mowforth/Munt[42]. Pretty's six ideal types of participation range from passive participation to self-mobilisation. Whereas in the former all the power and control lie with stakeholders outside the local community, in the latter they stay with the local community. Accordingly, the role of the external stakeholders ranges from that of the controller to that of the enabler. Moreover, it should not be overlooked that also *within* any given local community an imbalance of power is a common reality. Introducing new activities such as tourism contains the risk of even enlarging local elites' power. Zimmermann, by referring to Simmons[43], counters this risk by applying the concept of equality[44]. Equality[45] in participation, which together with involvement and efficiency makes up the three conditions required to reach equality, is the most effective instrument to limit local elitism and prevent community disruption. Therefore, according to Zimmermann, in all tourism projects, each different group or sector should be equally represented, regardless of e.g. gender, financial means or age.[46]

Community participation can be direct, e.g. through representatives in committees, or indirect, e.g. through public meetings. Whether direct or indirect, participatory approaches consume time and resources, in particular during the planning of a tourism product. But then again its implementation is usually easier and faster.[47] Not least, it has to be considered that, as Zimmermann stresses, a "lack of stakeholder participation is one of the main causes of project failure"[48].

Community-based tourism can be categorised either as another alternative tourism paradigm, such as sustainable tourism, or as a specification of the latter. The same is true for pro-poor tourism: this paradigm is definitely an alternative one, but it can also be seen as a further development of community-based tourism.

Pro-poor Tourism

Pro-poor tourism has a lot in common with the other two alternative tourism paradigms outlined above. But while sustainable tourism, at least in its early stage, focuses more on ecological sustainability, and community-based tourism focuses on the participation of the local community, pro-poor tourism refers explicitly to the potential of tourism to reduce poverty, i.e. "on maximising benefits for the poor"[49] by directly meeting their needs. People classified as "poor" are those who live under the widely used international poverty line of one US-Dollar a day.[50] This primarily economic approach usually does not apply a further distinction between the poorest, the poor and the less poor.

In contrast to sustainable tourism and community-based tourism, pro-poor tourism is clearly defined by DFID as tourism that "generates net benefits for the poor"[51], which simply means that the benefits have to exceed the costs. Although pro-poor tourism takes into account the social and ecological dimensions of sustainability as well, it clearly stresses the importance of economic benefits. Proponents like the British joint venture Pro-poor Tourism Partnership, being perhaps the most influential opinion leader in the debate, however, do not tire of repeating that pro-poor tourism focuses less on expanding tourism as a whole than on "unlocking opportunities" for the poor within it: "tilting the cake, not expanding it"[52] is the pursued strategy. The five principles on which this strategy is founded are detailed in Ashley et al.[53] Pros and cons of pro-poor tourism and the necessity to integrate pro-poor tourism both in the conventional tourism industry and in a broader development strategy aiming at poverty alleviation are discussed at length in Mowforth/Munt[54], Luger[55] and Ashley et al.[56]

Until the late 1990s, in the development policy debate it was assumed that the (environmental and social) costs of tourism usually would exceed its (economic) benefits. However, this widespread assumption was disproved by the *Sustainable Tourism and Poverty Elimination Study* commissioned by the Department for International Development[57] and the UNWTO study *Tourism and Poverty Alleviation*[58] at the latest. Based on the key finding of the latter, tourism being a primary export product of Less and Least Developed Countries,[59] UNWTO launched its *Sustainable Tourism – Eliminating Poverty* programme (ST-EP). This paradigm shift was finally accomplished by the joint signature of a Memorandum of Understanding by UNWTO and the Netherlands Development Organisation SNV, one of the strongest promoters of pro-poor tourism[60], in 2004[61].

Maybe the most important push factor for the success of the paradigm of pro-poor tourism is the strong link of UNWTO's ST-EP programme to the Millennium Development Goals (MDGs). As up to 2015 the MDGs were a good conceptual starting point for implementing any alternative tourism product, today the Sustainable Development Goals (SDGs) and the International Year of Sustainable Tourism for Development are a crucial reference. However, prior to putting into practice paradigms like sustainable tourism, community-based tourism or pro-poor tourism, they must be adapted to the site-specific reality. Therefore, first of all, it is imperative to formulate premises and limitations to bridge the gap between the theoretical discussion and the application of the theory to case-by-case real-world situations.

Premises and Limitations

All tourism paradigms are ideal types which do not exist in a pure form. This is particularly true for paradigms which follow a holistic approach. Therefore, it is not appropriate to regard a tourism paradigm as a rigid framework, but rather as an adaptive paradigm[62]. In the broad spectrum of sustainable tourism – approaches range from comprehensive to minimalist, hard to soft and strong to weak – one has to make concessions to the facts on the ground. Be it sustainable tourism, community-based tourism or pro-poor tourism, the potential of tourism to contribute to sustainable development e.g. of a whole country or just a single community has to be put into perspective. Weaver gets to the heart of the adaptive paradigm by stating that "sustainable tourism involves the minimization of negative impacts and the maximization of positive impacts"[63]. The same applies for community-based and pro-poor tourism by maximising the participation of the local community and the net benefits for the poor respectively.

Since "theory and practice do not always coincide"[64], the holistic approach in practice has to be given up. Aspiring to a "'balanced' form of development"[65], the proverbial middle path between the two poles of government-inspired mega-projects and community-inspired local projects founded on the principle of subsidiarity should be sought. The objectives of sustainable, community-based or pro-poor tourism might not be achieved in its purest form but they serve as fundamentals for the formulation of a guiding star, presented in the following box:

> Based on financial sustainability, sustainable community-based pro-poor tourism should lead to the maximisation of benefits and minimisation of costs in all dimensions of sustainability, namely environmental, social, cultural and economic, both on a spatial and temporal scale. Political sustainability – in other words the right of participation of all stakeholders in all phases of the product cycle – public-private partnership and the subsidiary advice of experts should contribute to the subjective well-being of the local community and its members as well as to the optimum satisfaction of the visitor requirements. Above all, the generation of net benefits for the "poor" should be the ultimate goal.

Box 1. Guiding star

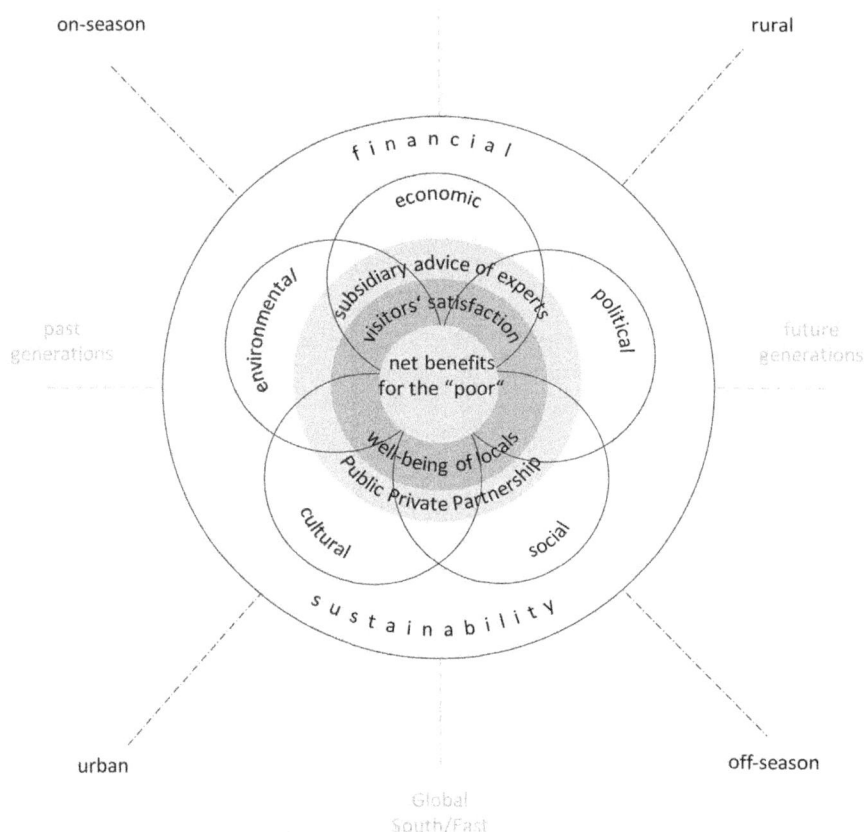

on-season

rural

financial

economic

subsidiary advice of experts

visitors' satisfaction

environmental

political

net benefits for the "poor"

past generations

future generations

well-being of locals

Public Private Partnership

cultural

social

sustainability

urban

off-season

Global South/East

Chart 1. Guiding star (developed by Adam)

Chart 1. shows the interrelation of the fundamentals of the guiding star which serves as paradigmatic framework to this paper. As a basis for the application of the guiding star to the Bhutanese reality, the following chapter provides an analysis of the country's unique way of development, which is also crucial for the analysis of tourism in Bhutan in the chapter Tourism in Bhutan.

Development in Bhutan

Looking back on the history of Bhutan in the 20th and 21st centuries, Ura, Director of the government think tank Centre for Bhutan Studies and GNH Research, identifies five sequential phases of transformation which have determined the development of the country since 1961[66]. From 1961 to 1973 (1), Bhutan focused on the establishment of international relations and on the construction of roads. The latter was then the basic requirement for expanding health, education and agricultural extension services between 1973 and 1983 (2), which in turn resulted in a considerable budgetary overspend. Generating revenue by investing in hydropower and energy-intensive industries became the backbone of the economic growth between 1983 and 1987 (3). Between 1987 and 1998 (4), Bhutan gave up isolation by expanding air connections and telecommunication networks. Finally, after 1998 (5), globalisation and democratisation have caught up with the reality of this long-time isolated and absolutist ruled kingdom.

Continuing this path of development from the perspective of a classical linear stages of growth model, the fifth phase might be considered as having concluded in 2013 with the holding of the second democratic elections and the entry into force of the 11th FYP. The sixth phase will likely be dominated by the country's striving for self-reliance and economic independence from India and international aid until 2018.

Since 2000, the development of Bhutan has not only been guided by the FYPs but also by a twenty-year perspective strategy called *Bhutan 2020: A Vision for Peace, Prosperity and Happiness*, developed by the Planning Commission of the Royal Government of Bhutan. This Vision Statement should provide long-term orientation and direction within these twenty years, while the respective short- and medium-term strategies should be set in the FYPs[67]. Vision 2020 should become a "useful reference in the course of planning [which] ensures the continuity of policies over the long term"[68]. After 2020, it will be the task of the third democratically elected government of Bhutan to verify if the country has achieved the highly ambitious development goals defined in the Vision 2020 under the former head of government, the fourth *Druk Gyalpo*.

Bhutan's path of development originates in, as Priesner – the previous programme officer of the United Nations Development Programme (UNDP) in Thimphu – stresses correctly, "one of the last truly indigenous development approaches"[69], not least because the political, social and economic environments were "simply too different to rate Bhutan's development performance in comparison with neighbouring countries"[70]. Ura specifies five causes, which led to the "take-off" of a country which in the early 1960s had more in common with a feudal medieval kingdom than with a modern constitutional monarchy: (1) first and foremost the *Druk Gyalpo*, who until 1998 was the guarantor of continuity and cohesiveness; (2) a favourable relationship between the country's wealth in natural resources, in particular hydropower, and its low population pressure; (3) a relatively efficient administrative body and a still cohesive community organisation; (4) long-term support of regional and international donors; and (5) finally the primacy of the Bhutanese culture. The latter, however, is – particularly since the entry into force of the Citizen Act of 1985 – more than controversial.[71]

But actually it was one "powerful vision"[72] which has led to an "astonishingly smooth and undistorted"[73] development, a vision which "evolved from the country's unique historical, geopolitical and sociological circumstances"[74] in the past and which determines its present and future: Gross National Happiness (GNH).

Gross National Happiness

Gross National Happiness (GNH) is the official development philosophy of Bhutan. In the eyes of the fifth *Druk Gyalpo* it simply signifies "Development with Values"[75], an approach, which should "secure a synergistic and harmonious balance between material well-being and the spiritual, emotional and cultural needs of an individual and society"[76].

The idea of GNH was born as in 1972 the fourth *Druk Gyalpo* declared that "Gross National Happiness is more important than Gross National Product"[77]. While there is no official definition of GNH and – in some measure – no common understanding of GNH at all,[78] it might be described as "a set of values that promote collective happiness as the end value of any development strategy"[79]. GNH is a holistic, balanced, collective, sustainable and equitable development approach. By giving priority to happiness, "progress should be viewed not only through the lens of economics but also from spiritual, social, cultural and ecological perspectives"[80], although, as the GNH Commission (GNHC) stresses, this does not "in any way exclude or deny the importance of economic growth"[81]. Nevertheless, the legal code of 1729 already states that "if the government cannot create happiness (*dekidk*) for its people, there is no purpose for the government to exist"[82]. Since 2008, the Constitution has bound the state "to promote those conditions that will enable the pursuit of Gross National Happiness" (Constitution, Art. 9, par. 2) and the maximisation of GNH has become the "all-encompassing and penultimate goal of development"[83] as GNHC proclaims in the 10th FYP.

The concept of GNH has its roots in the Buddhist tradition of the country; Buddhist thinking – or rather ethical and moral cosmology – inspired GNH, although it is not a religious development approach[84].

In Buddhist thinking, *happiness* stands rather for a constant, balanced and intrinsically motivated condition than for a situational, intensive and extrinsically motivated emotion. Therefore, it might have been more appropriate to use the word *contentment* instead[85]. Further, Buddhist teaching acknowledges that the individual cannot be happy or content if those around her or him are unhappy or discontent. Therefore, it is the responsibility of the government to create the political, social and economic environment – beyond the satisfaction of basic needs – for the people to pursue happiness and to translate GNH into policy[86]. This is why RGoB e.g. in the 10th FYP strives to put into practice GNH by focusing on the following four pillars: (1) sustainable and equitable socio-economic development; (2) environmental conservation; (3) preservation and promotion of culture; and (4) good governance. These four pillars are specified by nine dimensions. While three of them – living standard, health and education – are traditional domains of public policy and two – ecological diversity and good governance – have become common in other countries too, the remaining four – psychological wellbeing, time use, community vitality and cultural diversity – are endogenous dimensions of GNH[87].[88] However, Bhutan's national development goals contradicted neither the international Millennium Development Goals (MDGs) nor the regional SAARC Development Goals. On the contrary, the government has set even higher national goals compared to the

MDGs and the SAARC Development Goals[89] as well as to the Sustainable Development Goals (SDGs).

GNH, as Ura rightly concludes, "tries to take the country from being a late starter in modernization directly to a sustainable society"[90]. In this way, the main challenge for Bhutanese society and its members will be to "fit a lifestyle that reflects a balance between tradition and modernisation, between materialism and spiritualism, and between commodity wealth and quality of life"[91]. The five guiding principles of development – economic self-reliance, preservation of environment, regionally balanced development, decentralisation and community empowerment as well as cultural preservation[92] – may help Bhutan to find and follow its middle path, but they might also be a hindrance as is best illustrated by the case of the Bhutanese identity.

Identity

Bhutan experienced a profound process of nation-building: on the one hand because of external pressure as a result of the annexation of Tibet by China in 1951 and the suppression of the Khampas' revolt in 1959, on the other hand by virtue of the internal unification of the nation by Shabdrung Ngawang Namgyal in the 17th century and the establishment of the Wangchuck dynasty in 1907[93]. These historical facts, along with the almost entire absence of foreign domination, as well as having Buddhism and feudalism as everlasting cornerstones of the traditional socioeconomic order, resulted in "an exceptionally strong consciousness of political, social and cultural identity"[94], "an incomparably stronger sense of identity than in western societies"[95]. GNH, as stated above, may be the "all-encompassing and penultimate *goal of development [emphasis added]*"[96] but the "overarching goal [...] that stands above all others"[97] is something else, namely "*to ensure the future independence, sovereignty and security [emphasis in original]*"[98] of Bhutan. Identity – complemented by GNH being the "single unifying concept of development"[99] – is the most important of the guiding principles and plays a key role in Vision 2020:

> "*Our independence, sovereignty and security will continue to be dependent upon the assertion of our distinctive Bhutanese identity. This has provided the key to our survival as a nation state in the past and it will continue to be so in the future. This requires us to continue to articulate an unambiguous cultural imperative in all that we do and to actively promote an awareness and appreciation of the continued relevance of our cultural heritage [...].*"[100]

Setting the culture of the Ngalop as *Leitkultur* of Bhutan goes back to the unification of the nation by Shabdrung Ngawang Namgyal in the 17th century[101]. Since then, identity, sovereignty and security are perceived as the magic triangle which guarantees the survival of the Bhutanese nation[102]. Today, the culture of the Ngalop is omnipresent, ranging from language and architecture to the national dress, *gho* (for men) and *kira* (for women). It is not the purpose of this paper to examine either the positive or the negative impacts of this cultural imperative on the development of the country, but rather to stress that it is an essential element of Bhutanese reality. Priesner underlines that the development of Bhutan, particularly in view of the many trouble spots in the region, was and still is a remarkable success. According to Priesner, the only huge mistake in the success story of this small Himalayan Kingdom is the dealing with the still very controversial question of the *Lhotsampa* in Southern Bhutan, which is still anything but resolved.[103] The anthology *Bhutan: Aspects of culture and development*[104] edited by Aris/Hutt gives a valuable insight into the so-called "Bhutanese cultural crisis"[105], when the country at the end of the 1980s and the beginning of the 1990s experienced "one of the most critical moments of its history"[106]. Details on the conflict in Southern Bhutan can be found in Obrecht[107] and Luger[108].

Socioeconomic challenges of Bhutan

The development of Bhutan has its strengths and weaknesses, which is also true for GNH. However, it is remarkable that a small country like Bhutan has become internationally known and respected thanks to its endogenous development approach. Since the beginning of the 21st century and in particular since 2008 when Jigmi Yoer Thinley – the first-ever democratically elected Prime Minister of Bhutan and a strong promoter of GNH – took office, GNH has gone international. Since then, several regional and international conferences on GNH were held. In 2012, 20th March was declared the *International Day of Happiness* by the General Assembly of the United Nations[109] and the first *World Happiness Report*[110] was released. The United Nations even asked Bhutan – supported by an International Expert Working Group – to elaborate a post MDGs development paradigm, called the New Development Paradigm. The report *Happiness: Towards a New Development Paradigm* was submitted to the United Nations in December 2013[111].

Even though the General Assembly recognises "the need for a more inclusive, equitable and balanced approach to economic growth that promotes sustainable development, poverty eradication, happiness and the well-being of all peoples" and is conscious that "the pursuit of happiness is a fundamental human goal"[112], Bhutan, as Dorji rightly emphasises, "was not – and is not – in a position to teach or preach GNH [and it] has certainly not worked out the solutions to the world's problems"[113]. But, he continues, "I think we have opened up an amazing conversation"[114].

As a member of the increasingly globalised and interdependent world, Bhutan is not and cannot be a "GNH bubble in a GDP-centred world"[115]. That has been proven not only by the political and cultural challenges which the country is facing until today but also by the socioeconomic ones. This chapter is based on the personal experiences of the author during three months of field study – in particular countless informal chats and formal conversations with Bhutanese in private and professional contexts – and is enriched by two years of academic study of development and tourism in Bhutan.

The most obvious challenge which Bhutan has faced since 1961 is its dependence on India. India is not only the exclusive buyer of electricity and main provider of petroleum products, consumer goods and food, but also by far the most important donor and creditor of development aid. Further, Indian labour, skilled or unskilled, dominates the secondary sector, in particular the construction industry that has boomed for decades. It is commonly known that the Bhutanese hydropower plants were financed by the Government of India and built by Indian migrant labour, following Indian construction plans and mainly using building materials provided by Indian companies. As a consequence, a large portion of the development aid and credits Bhutan receives directly flows back to India, generating, at least during the years of construction, more revenue for the national economy of India than for that of Bhutan. Mathou even goes one step further and stresses the link between economic dependency and the fear of a possible cultural dilution: "[o]n the one hand, the kingdom cannot do without foreign inputs, either as imported labour or development funds. On the other hand, it must limit its exposure to the outside world to prevent a dilution of its culture"[116].

Concerning domestic matters, rural-urban migration, youth unemployment and lack of jobs in the tertiary sector are the three main challenges which are highly interrelated. Over the last decades, Bhutan, in particular its two major cities Thimphu and Phuentsholing, has experienced an enormous urbanisation[117]. Although Obrecht found out that the electrification of the rural areas of Bhutan has led to a significant decrease in the desire to migrate from the villages to the urban areas, the "bright lights" of the cities have not lost their attraction, as can be construed from the rapid urbanisation of the Thimphu Valley[118]. Many Bhutanese parents, if they do not migrate for working reasons themselves, send their children to high school or college in Thimphu hoping that after graduation they will become white-collar workers, at best civil servants who will be able to send remittances back home. Blue-collar jobs instead are rarely honoured and few Bhutanese strive for a job in the secondary sector which, as mentioned above, is traditionally dominated by Indian labour migrants. Reducing this imbalance of demand for blue-collar workers in the secondary sector and the supply of white-collar workers in the tertiary sector will be one more challenge for the new government, not least because it made the pre-election promise of reaching full employment for the youth[119].

Just like self-reliance, decentralisation of the political, cultural, social and economic life of the Bhutanese has become a key word in the debate on the future development of the country. Creating jobs in the tertiary sector outside the urban centres has the potential to reduce internal migration and youth unemployment. All of these challenges have one thing in common: tourism, in particular sustainable, community-based and pro-poor tourism, has the potential to foster overcoming them and reducing the economic dependence on India. The chapter Tourism and Development in Bhutan explains how tourism is theoretically planned on the national level to become a means of development. Beforehand, the tourism system of Bhutan is characterised in the following by setting out its particularities.

Tourism in Bhutan

The coronation of the fourth *Druk Gyalpo* Jigme Singye Wangchuck in 1974 marks the beginning of tourism in Bhutan. 150 non-Indian foreigners, until that day the largest number ever permitted to enter the kingdom, attended the three-day ceremony in Thimphu[120]. In the same year, the first group of so-called dollar paying visitors (hereafter referred to as tourists) obtained permission to visit the valleys of Paro and Thimphu[121]. At the end of 1974, 287 tourists had travelled to the long isolated kingdom[122].

Now, more than four decades later, Bhutan is regarded as "one of the most exclusive travel destinations in the world"[123]. This last Mahayana Buddhist Kingdom is perfectly designed as a brand which projects the image of a "unique, exotic, cultural and unspoilt destination"[124] and which strengthens the Bhutanese national identity[125]. Tourism contributes to the maximisation of GNH and, first and foremost, generates revenues, in particular foreign exchange[126]. Before examining the interrelation of tourism and development, one has to understand the tourism system of Bhutan and its unique basis in the tourism policy of *high value – low impact*.

Tourism System

Right from the beginning, Bhutan has been aware that uncontrolled and unrestricted tourism could have a negative impact on its "pristine environment" and "unique culture"[127]. Subsequently, long before the concept of sustainability was first mentioned in the 5th FYP (1981–1986),[128] a middle path between cultural preservation and environmental conservation on the one hand and socioeconomic development and revenue generation on the other had to be found: the famous tourism policy *high value – low volume* was born.

At the beginning of tourism in Bhutan in 1974, the basic idea of this policy was the indirect limitation of the number of tourist arrivals by charging a relatively high daily fee while offering an organised – and controllable – travel package (see below). These days and particularly in view of the political debate about the future of the country's tourism policy, one recognises that *high value – low volume* is more and more replaced by *high value – low impact*. In the opinion of the author of this paper, the semantic difference between *low volume* and *low impact* mirrors the upcoming paradigm shift from exclusiveness – including limitation – to the precautionary principle, meaning that a low number of tourists does not automatically equate low impact on environment and culture.[129] In this context it has to be clarified that it is not true that Bhutan is formally limiting tourism by law.

Nevertheless, in the past tourism was in a sense limited: During the 7th FYP (1992–1997) the government *increased* the maximum number of tourists to 4,000 per year.[130] The 7th FYP, though, is the only one which determines any maximum of tourist arrivals; there is no other official document known to the author which indicates a pre-4,000 maximum. However, it is essential to stress that RGoB increased this maximum to 4,000 not in order to *limit* tourist arrivals but to *enable* the attraction of more tourists. For decades, however, tourism development was sluggish and tourist arrivals did not exceed this ceiling before 1995.[131] One reason may be that until 1982 tourism was limited to Western Bhutan, not least because of a lack of tourist and basic infrastructure outside the valleys of Paro and Thimphu.[132] Another cause might be that the state-owned airline Druk Air did not begin operation before 1983, with only three flights a week from Paro with one 18-seater Dornier aircraft.[133] and that entering the country by road via Phuentsholing was – and is even today – arduous and time consuming.

Tourism development changed fundamentally in 1991 with the privatisation of the tourism industry and the creation of the regulatory body Tourism Authority of Bhutan (TAB). Before that, Bhutan Tourism Corporation (BTC), a fully government owned enterprise, had held an absolute monopoly on tourism business, undertaking all tourism activities and maintaining nearly all tourism infrastructure:[134] until 1991, all tourists had to come as guests of BTC[135] – or one of its predecessor organisations.

TAB was then renamed Department of Tourism (DOT)[136] and later, after having been granted autonomy in 2008, reconstituted as Tourism Council of Bhutan (TCB)[137]. Today, TCB is mandated by RGoB with the management and development of the Bhutanese tourism industry[138]. As a regulatory authority, its primary responsibilities are (1) to "formulate, implement and update a national tourism policy and strategy" and (2) to "develop and implement relevant tourism guidelines and regulatory measures"[139].

The gap between the now private tourism industry and the public regulatory body TCB was closed in 2000 by the foundation of the Association of Bhutanese Tour Operators (ABTO), a Civil Society Organisation (CSO) representing the tour operators of Bhutan[140]. ABTO was followed by three other interest groups: the Hotel and Restaurant Association of Bhutan (HRAB) in 2007,[141] the Guides Association of Bhutan (GAB) in 2009[142] and the Handicraft Association of Bhutan (HAB) in 2011[143].

Today, the core stakeholders of the Bhutanese tourism system – Druk Air[144], TCB, ABTO and, to a lesser extent, HRAB, GAB and HAB – are closely cooperating to put the tourism policy into practice. *High value – low impact* does not only serve the "purpose of creating an image of exclusivity and high-yield"[145], it is indeed a lived reality in Bhutan. The tourism system of Bhutan is surprisingly well established and the guidelines of TCB, published on its website, are followed accordingly. Further, rules and regulations for single stakeholders like the tour operators were set at the end of the 1990s and include details such as the (out-of-date) *Schedule of Tariff for International Tourists*, the *Codes of Conduct for Tour Guides* as well as the *Minimum Meal Entitlement per Tourist*[146].

It has to be stressed that the Bhutanese tourism system is based on a truly indigenous tourism industry which is founded on the principle of sustainability and nationality. The importance of the latter becomes apparent, for example, in the *Rules & Regulations for Tour Operations in Bhutan* stating right at the beginning that all tour operators and their employees must be Bhutanese nationals and, to foster the Bhutanese image and identity, shall always wear the national dress, meaning full *kira* for women and full *gho* for men[147]. This applies in particular to the guides who are considered as "ambassador[s] of the country"[148] and mediators between the host culture and its guests. Regarding the principle of sustainability and according to TCB, tourism must be "environmentally and ecologically friendly, socially and culturally acceptable and economically viable"[149]. To achieve this ambitious target, RGoB has developed a unique concept: the so-called minimum daily package.

Each and every tourist has to pre-book a minimum daily package through a licensed Bhutanese tour operator or one of its international partners. This package includes (1) a 3-star accommodation; (2) all meals; (3) a licensed Bhutanese tour guide for the extent of the stay; (4) all internal transports (excluding internal flights); and, for trekking tourists, camping equipment and pack animals. Further, it comprises all internal taxes and charges and a royalty of USD 65 (see chapter Tourism and Development in Bhutan). Depending on tour group size and season, the minimum selling prices are set between USD 200 and USD 290 per tourist per night.[150] The total amount has to be transferred in advance to TCB in USD which, after receiving the full payment, including an USD 40 visa fee, issues the tourist visa[151].

The misunderstanding of the tourism policy *high value – low impact* might be the reason why many people believe that Bhutan is still limiting its tourist arrivals by law. The only limiting factor for tourist arrivals may be the lack, overstrain or interruption of the basic and touristic infrastructure. Particularly during peak season in spring and autumn, Druk Air, tour operators, hotels and restaurants, as well as guides, may work at full capacity and unfavourable weather – not only during the monsoon in summer – may cause landslides blocking roads or delays and cancellation of Druk Air flights.

It is true that in Bhutan individual tourism in the proper sense is a *de facto* forbidden practice. Every individual tourist is, like all tour groups, accompanied by a guide and a driver, making her/him a so-called "one-member group" or "group of one". However, by pre-booking a fully customised travel package, which still gives leeway to changes in situ, she/he enjoys a relatively high degree of individualisation of her/his trip.

The policy *high value – low impact* is applied to all dollar paying or international tourists. Not more than three countries are excluded from the international segment: India, Bangladesh and the Maldives. Citizens of these countries visiting Bhutan are referred to as regional visitors (hereafter referred to as regional tourists) who do not require a tourist visa and therefore are exempt from paying a minimum tourism tariff[152]. Moreover, for regional tourists from India and Bangladesh, as well as for Bhutanese citizens, Druk Air offers concessional airfares which are considerably lower than the rates for international tourists.[153] The reason for the different dealing with international and regional visitors lays in an open border policy which Bhutan shares with its regional partners, first and foremost with India, not least due to economic interests.

The Bhutanese tourism system has made the country a unique tourism brand which is marketed above all as synonymous to happiness. "Bhutan. Happiness is a place", the new slogan of TCB and the position statement of the brand, says a big banner welcoming the visitors at the International Airport of Paro. Bhutan itself has become a Unique Selling Proposition (USP) whose comparative advantage lays in its perception as a "[…] Himalayan Buddhist country with a unique living culture, pristine environment and a noble development philosophy [which] is regarded as a destination that combines the best of culture and nature"[154]. In order to follow the already mentioned middle path and "[m]indful of the problems that beset neighboring Nepal when she suddenly ended her isolation and let Westerners flood in"[155], Bhutan sticks to the precautionary principle in tourism. In marketing, the tourism policy of *high value – low impact* is translated into practice as target marketing. By attempting to attract a specific market segment that is believed to provide far more advantages than disadvantages for the tourist destination, Bhutan, as Weaver puts it correctly, "tr[ies] to cultivate a 'quality', 'high end' or 'upscale' tourism sector by attracting relatively small numbers of high-spending, older and well-educated tourists who generate large revenue flows but are perceived as being less likely to behave inappropriately"[156].[157] This demand management approach, just like the tourism policy as a whole, aims to achieve a sustainable balance between supply and demand, push and pull factors, as well as quality and quantity of tourist arrivals.

Profile of Tourism

First of all it has to be stressed that the profile of tourism is influenced by both extrinsic and intrinsic factors. The former are pre-set primarily by the country's geography, that is to say its location – making it a long-distance destination – along with its climate and its topography. Bhutan's cultural and natural heritage, the basic infrastructure on site as well as its development approach, GNH, are the other extrinsic factors defining the profile. All these extrinsic factors, except GNH, turn Bhutan into a seasonal destination.

The intrinsic factors, on the other hand, result from the tourism policy *high value – low impact*, designed by political decision-makers. Following the precautionary principle, the combination of the minimum daily package and target marketing not only guarantees a favourable ratio of tourist arrivals to tourism earnings but also generates high profits for the tour operators. In the private sector, they are the ones who profit most from the Bhutanese tourism system. The partial lack of tourism infrastructure, like the absence of three-star-accommodation in almost half of the *dzongkhags*, and a still little diversified tourist offer are the other crucial factors intrinsic to the tourism system.

It is the meshing of these extrinsic and intrinsic factors which gives rise to the brand *Bhutan* created to promote the country as the last Shangri-la in the world: *Bhutan. Happiness is a place.* The triad of the brand *Bhutan*, the seasonality of the destination and the Bhutanese tourism policy form the unique profile of tourism in Bhutan.

In conclusion, this profile is characterised firstly by the accessibility of a limited number of tourist attractions which is easy for cultural and difficult for natural sights. The *Leitmotiv* "time is money" makes it easier for the "average tourists to Bhutan" to exclude natural tourist attractions from the dense (cultural) travel program. These elderly and wealthy "average tourists" visit the country mainly in spring and autumn concentrating their short-holiday trip to Western (and Central) Bhutan and are supposedly (highly) satisfied with the service they receive.

All these characteristics that make up the profile of tourism make Bhutan a "once in a lifetime destination", a destination that definitely has to be experienced once – but not necessarily twice.

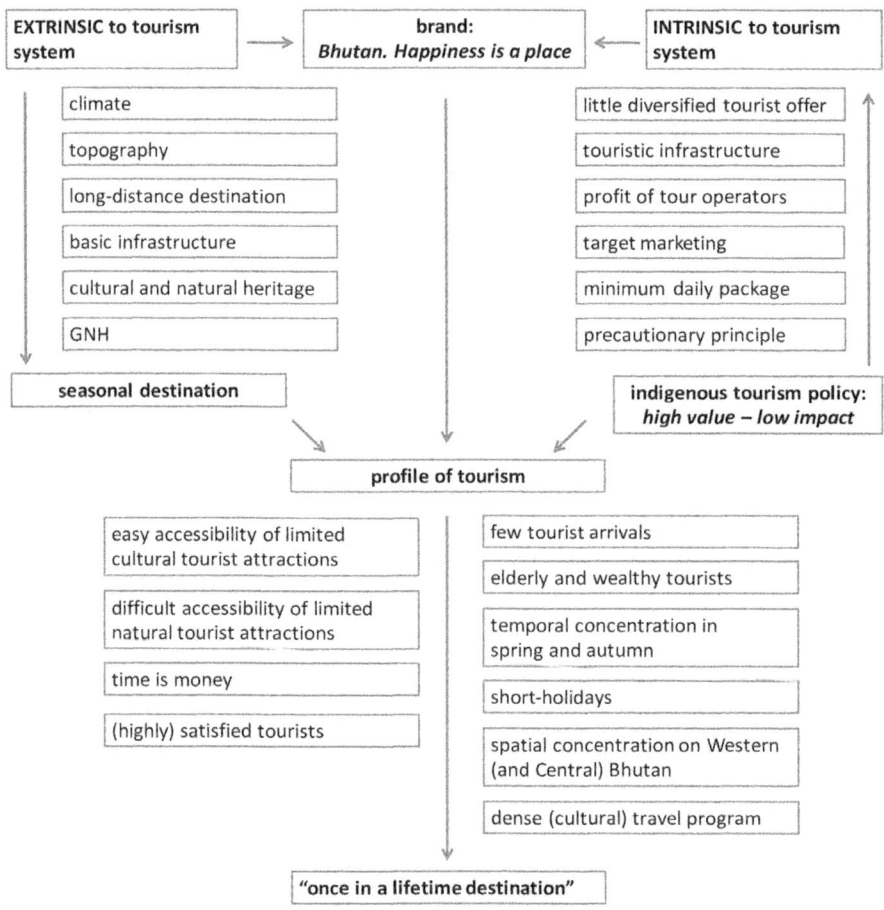

Chart 2. Profile of Tourism in Bhutan (developed by Adam)

In general and particularly in comparison to countries in the region, first and foremost Nepal, the Bhutanese tourism system performs well today. Nevertheless, the profile of tourism in Bhutan proves that both tourism arrivals and earnings have to be spread significantly more spatially, temporally and, not least, socially within the country and among its inhabitants. RGoB, GNHC and TCB have recognised this necessity and determined relevant objectives and strategies. The latter should not only make the Bhutanese tourism sector more competitive, they should also guarantee that tourism contributes to the sustainable development of the kingdom. The objectives Bhutan has set and the strategies which will be employed to achieve them are examined in the following chapter.

Tourism and Development in Bhutan

One means to foster the development of Bhutan via tourism earnings is the royalty. As stated above, each minimum daily package includes a royalty fee of USD 65. This taxation is earmarked for (1) free education, (2) free healthcare and (3) poverty alleviation for the population of Bhutan[158]. In 2016, more than 27.5% of USD 73.74 million of direct gross earnings generated by international tourism were levied as royalty[159]. In other words, direct financial contribution of tourism to the sustainable development of the country reached USD 20.28 million.

But the contribution of tourism to the development of Bhutan goes far beyond this royalty. Tourism is an integral part of the interrelation of development and the already examined magic triangle of identity, sovereignty and security. The vision of TCB gets to the heart of it by seeking "[t]o foster a vibrant industry as a positive force in the conservation of environment, promotion of cultural heritage, safeguarding sovereign status of the Nation for significantly contributing to Gross National Happiness"[160]. Leading on from this vision, objectives and strategies for the tourism sector are established in the 10th FYP.

Tourism and the 10th Five Year Plan, GNHC

The core objective of the 10th FYP is poverty reduction.[161] To achieve broad-based growth, RGoB, represented by GNHC, developed 101 development programmes,[162] two of them emphasise the strengths of tourism: tourism provides employment, generates foreign exchange and has "contributed immensely to strengthening Bhutan's image and identity around the world"[163]. Both are coordinated by TCB and implemented in coordination with *dzongkhags*, *gewogs* and other relevant agencies, in particular with ABTO[164].

To guarantee the long term sustainability of tourism, RGoB recognises its weaknesses which have already been stressed in the analysis of the tourism sector above: spatial, temporal and social concentration. Moreover, RGoB identifies a general lack of tourism knowledge among the stakeholders of the sector. However, this issue is not examined in the analysis – not least since in 2012 tourists hardly complained about the quality of tourism services. To address these weaknesses, the 10th FYP sets nine specific objectives which should be achieved by employing 16 strategies. In order to systematise these mere listings, the author of this paper presents the objectives and strategies most relevant to tourism and development in the following chart. While two objectives are considered to be strategies as well, the other six objectives and the five strategies most important to the author are put into relation to each other.

Objectives		Strategies
Promote Bhutan as a unique, exotic, cultural and unspoilt destination		
Improve the regional and local spread of benefits	→	Promote tourism in eastern and southern Bhutan
Improve the quality of services; develop and upgrade tourism human resources	→	Train the next generation of tourism professionals in the country and [sic] according to international standards through the Hotel Tourism and Management Training Institute (HTMTI)
Diversify and develop new tourism products	→	Create new, off season products and/or implement a differentiated seasonal pricing policy
Increase community participation	→	Promote community based and rural tourism
Broaden the base of demand	→	Target new source markets and groups
Improve infrastructure		

Chart 3. Objectives and strategies of the 10ᵗʰ FYP in tourism.[165]

These objectives shall be reached by implementing two development programmes, namely the *Sustainable Tourism Development Programme* (TCB/01) and the *Hotel & Tourism Management Training Institute* (TCB/02). The costs of the former amount to approx. USD 3.1 million, the latter comes to approx. USD 8.7 million.[166] Both are entirely funded by external financing[167]. The results frameworks of the programmes are detailed as follows:

	Impact	Outcome	Output	Projects/Activities
TCB/01	Contribution to national revenue and improve livelihoods of the community	Increase in number of tourists and tourism income	Off-set seasonality and regionally balanced tourism	Development of new and innovative products
			Community aware of tourism benefits and adverse impacts	Awareness building
				Infrastructure development and other services
			Quality infrastructure serviceable	
			Diversified tourism	Research, marketing and development of market strategy
			Tourist happy with services	Hospitality training services

	Impact	Outcome	Output	Projects/Activities
TCB/02	International standard quality services provided in the hotels and hospitality services	Trained youths employed	HTMTI operational	Infrastructure development including hotel Recreation facilities and other services

Chart 4. Results frameworks of TCB/01 and TCB/02.[168]

Although poverty reduction is the core objective of the 10th FYP, self-reliance and decentralisation are the key words of the debate on the future development of Bhutan and its tourism sector. A wide range of activities which could contribute to sustainable, pro-poor or community-based tourism should not only counteract rural-urban migration, in particular of the youth, but also reduce the leakage of tourism income to Thimphu and to India. TCB puts it this way in its *Tourism Strategy and Development Plans 2013–2018*:

(a) *maximising,* to the greatest possible extent, economic benefits and opportunities flowing to Bhutanese people – especially in terms of income and employment generation and regional development around the country; and,

(b) *minimising,* to the greatest possible extent, leakage of the tourist dollar out of the country through imports of meats, grains, vegetables, fruits, alcohol and other beverages, confectionary, toiletries, cosmetics, labour etc. that form component parts of its tourism industry.[169]

These plans are a response of TCB to the objectives and strategies set in the 10th FYP. Although in 2013 it was still a draft – since it was not officially approved by RGoB yet – in the tourism sector the plans of TCB were already accepted as framework for the operation of tourism business, which is why they are essential for the future development of tourism in Bhutan.

Tourism Strategy and Development Plans 2013–2018, TCB

Developed in 2012 with support of UNWTO, the *Tourism Strategy and Development Plans 2013–2018* of TCB aim to combine existing and new policies as well as current thinking about tourism in Bhutan. Designed as a planning and reference document, they should provide the basic direction for the planning process of future objectives and strategies.[170]

The overall objective of TCB is to make Bhutan a "premium standalone, world-renowned and year-round destination with a geographically spread product base and industry practices that align with the pillars of Gross National Happiness"[171] by 2018. To achieve this goal, a *Product Development Plan,* a *Marketing and Communication*

Plan as well as an *Institutional Development Plan* were set up. By focusing on the development of new tourism products, TCB sets its priorities clearly on the first plan which in turn focuses on three strategic recommendations: (1) position Bhutan as a carbon neutral destination; (2) develop cycle-tours and mountain-biking; and (3) develop eco-lodges and nature-based tours. These recommendations form the backbone of the *Development Plan*[172]. For this paper, the other two plans are not as important as the *Product Development Plan*, they are just mentioned for the sake of completeness.

To be successful, tourism planners have to follow the tourism strategies of RGoB and the strategic recommendations of TCB. The most relevant criteria for developing a new tourism product are summarised in the following box.

Tourism strategies of RGoB

---

promote Bhutan as a unique, exotic, cultural and unspoilt destination

promote tourism in Eastern and Southern Bhutan

create new, off season products

promote community based and rural tourism

target new source markets and groups

improve infrastructure

Strategic recommendations of TCB

---

position Bhutan as a carbon neutral destination

develop cycle-tours and mountain-biking

develop eco-lodges and nature-based tours

Chart 5. Tourism strategies of RGoB and strategic recommendations of TCB

In general, all stakeholders of the tourism sector in Bhutan – including the multitude of foreign development partners like the Austrian Development Agency (ADA) – have to align their activities with the objectives of the FYP and of TCB. To tourism planners, the findings of this paper reveal the "ideal" tourism product for Bhutan, which is defined in the box below. This "ideal" serves less as a blueprint than as an ideal in the literal sense of providing what tourism planners need to strive for.

The "ideal" tourism product for Bhutan is a new off-season nature or sport tourism product which generates benefits for rural communities, particularly to its "poor" members in Eastern or Southern Bhutan. The low carbon tourism product minimises the negative impact on the environment and increases community participation while it satisfies younger tourists to an extent that they stay longer in the region or even come back to the country.

Box 2. "Ideal" tourism product of Bhutan

Sustainable Tourism in Practice

Before developing a concrete tourism product under the paradigm of sustainable community-based pro-poor tourism, it has to be examined whether the guiding star is in accordance with the tourism development programmes of the country concerned or not. In other words, whether theory and practice, paradigm and reality, go together. If yes, it can considerably contribute to the successful implementation of a tourism product.

In Bhutan, the tourism development programmes of RGoB and TCB and in particular the tourism policy *high value – low impact* are a lived reality. Indeed, the profile of tourism and the tourism development programmes interact with each other; hence the examination of the latter has to be completed by elements of the profile. In the following, the fundamentals of the guiding star (Box 1) are analysed and compared to the objectives of RGoB and TCB.

Sustainability in all its facets is not only the main concern of the guiding star but also of RGoB and TCB and is therefore omnipresent in all official documents regarding tourism development. Although not rarely used as an umbrella term, its key message is the maximisation of (economic) benefits and minimisation of (economic) costs through touristic activities[173]. The other two classical dimensions – environmental and social sustainability – are not explicitly mentioned as often as the economic one. Nevertheless the emphasis on community participation e.g. in the 10th FYP[174] or on the conservation of the environment e.g. in the vision of TCB[175] clearly stresses how important they are to policy makers in Bhutan, not least since both are pillars of GNH of which pursuit is protected by the Constitution (Constitution Art. 9, par. 2).

Tourism in Bhutan is an unequally spread economic activity in spatial, temporal and social terms, a fact which determines its profile and which RoGB and TCB have been striving to counteract for years. TCB's overall objective and three of RGoB's tourism objectives directly address this imbalance, while one of the latter, increasing community participation, aims at also guaranteeing the political sustainability of tourism. In this dimension Bhutan has made considerable progress with the establishment of TCB in 2008, which fosters public-private partnership and which provides expertise to the stakeholders of the tourism system.

The subjective well-being of the local community and its members is not an explicit tourism objective of RGoB or TCB, but previous experiences have shown that it often goes hand in hand with objective well-being, commonly referred to as community development (e.g. better nutrition, sanitation or education). Further, psychological wellbeing is one of the nine dimensions of GNH, the official development philosophy of Bhutan.

Optimum visitor satisfaction, however, is not even implicitly mentioned by either RGoB or TCB, a fact which can be seen less as a disregard for the needs of the visitors than as an already high level of visitor satisfaction, proven year after year by the data provided by the annual *Tourism Monitor*[176]. Poverty reduction, in other words generation of net benefits for the poor, is in turn a main concern of RGoB, which made this ultimate goal of the guiding star the core objective of the 10th FYP.

The accordance of the developed guiding star of sustainable, community-based pro-poor tourism with the tourism development programmes in Bhutan proves that there is no formal reason why tourism planners who apply the guiding star as a paradigmatic framework should not be able to make a fitting tourism project a reality, provided that she or he properly assesses the intrinsic and extrinsic factors which determine the profile of tourism in Bhutan.

When putting theory into practice, the unique profile of Bhutanese tourism may be seen as an advantage or a disadvantage; in any case, it is a challenge for tourism planners and each tourism product has to be tailored to the Bhutanese reality. This is particularly evident keeping in mind the tourism policy *high value – low impact* which is – at least in foreseeable future – an unalterable factor just as most of the extrinsic ones, even though it might be questioned at times.

Conclusions and Reflexions

This paper shows that each tourism project has to make concessions to the facts on the ground. Even if perfectly planned, in theory as well as in practice, the development of a tourism offer cannot be linear, particularly not when the planners seek to include as many stakeholders as possible. In order to success, the most important premise is to put effort into political sustainability, which in turn would have a positive impact on the subsidiary relationship of external experts with local community as well as on the level of visitor satisfaction. The most important limitation is that the poorest members of a society hardly ever profit directly from tourism. Bhutan is no exception, although the royalty partly rebalances this fact. The notion of "poor" has to be redefined in the context of tourism in Bhutan, whereas those who are most vulnerable to the socioeconomic challenges of Bhutan – namely rural-urban migration, youth unemployment and lack of jobs in the tertiary sector – should be set as the target group.

As with almost all human activities, tourism too has its pros and cons. But is tourism itself in the end primarily advantageous or disadvantageous to the sustainable development of Bhutan? Firstly, tourism as an economic activity in the tertiary sector can reduce the economic dependence on India and can foster the self-reliance of Bhutan. It has to be kept in mind that, unquestionably, many consumer goods required for satisfying the demands of tourists must be imported from, or at least, via India. This ranges from food and beverages to trekking equipment and bicycles, not to mention vehicles and fuel. It is worth noting that these goods have to be imported anyhow, since Bhutan lacks a diversified manufacturing industry. Tourism dollars which do not leak out to India generate employment and tax revenue, particularly through the royalty, which is earmarked, as already stated, for free education, free healthcare and poverty alleviation. This tax revenue contributes to the government's income, which in turn depends less on earning generated by hydropower. On a national level, it has to be remembered that hydropower is becoming a main concern for environmentalists while tourism is regarded as a more environmental friendly economic activity. However, a positive evaluation of the overall environmental performance of tourism in Bhutan is doubtful since the country is a long-haul destination for most tourists.

Secondly, creating jobs in the tertiary sector can reduce youth unemployment and, if created in rural Bhutan, rural-urban migration. This fosters the decentralisation of political, cultural, social and economic life. Thirdly, the indigenous tourism industry, with all its restrictions, creates a sense of identity even if the cultural imperative set by the culture of the Ngalop as *Leitkultur* of Bhutan has to be questioned.

By merely concentrating on the tourism sector, it should not be forgotten that RGoB considers tourism as just another means to achieve the core objective of the FYPs, namely poverty reduction leading up to 2013 and self-reliance from 2014 onwards. In fact, all FYPs ultimately aim at the magic triangle which is perceived as having been the guarantor for the survival of the Bhutanese nation since its unification under Shabdrung Ngawang Namgyal in the 17th century: identity, sovereignty and security. Any human activity, touristic or not, which counteracts this magic triangle will have little prospect of success.

Notes

1   Adam, Gerhard (2014): *Sustainable pro-poor tourism in Bhutan*. Master's Thesis, University of Graz.
2   Cf. Fennell, David A. (2006): *Tourism Ethics*. Clevedon/Buffalo/Toronto: Channel View Publications (Aspects of Tourism 30), p. 12; Mowforth, Martin/Munt, Ian (2003): *Tourism and Sustainability. Development and New Tourism in the Third World*. Abingdon/New York: Routledge, p. 2.
3   Cf. Weaver, David (2006): *Sustainable Tourism. Theory and practice*. Oxford: Elsevier Butterworth-Heinemann, p. 15.
4   Butler, Richard (1998): *Sustainable Tourism – Looking Backwards in order to Progress?*, In: Hall, Michael C./Lew Alan A. (eds.): Sustainable Tourism. A Geographical Perspective. New York: Longman, pp. 25–34, p. 28.
5   Cf. Cater, Erlet/Lowman (1998): *Himalayan Tourism on the Sustainable Trail? An Introduction*. In: East, Patricia/Inmann, Karin/Luger, Kurt (eds.): Sustainability in Mountain Tourism. Perspectives for the Himalayan Countries. Delhi/Innsbruck: Book Faith India/Studienverlag, pp. 1–14, p. 3.
6   Cf. Zimmermann, Friedrich (1998): *Nature, Society and the Economy in Partnership. European Perspective in Mountain Tourism*. In: East, Patricia/Inmann, Karin/Luger, Kurt (eds.): Sustainability in Mountain Tourism, pp. 71–91, p. 72.
7   Cf. Briassoulis, Helen (2008): *Sustainable Tourism and the Question of the Commons*. In: Page, Stephen/Connell, Joanne (eds.): Sustainable Tourism. Critical Concepts in the Social Sciences, Vol. 1 Evolution and Context of Sustainable Tourism. Abingdon/New York: Routledge, pp. 481–503, p. 497.
8   Page, Stephen/Connell, Joanne (2008): *General Introduction. The Evolution and Development of Sustainable Tourism. Progress and Prospects*. In: Page/Connell (eds.): Sustainable Tourism, pp. 1–20, p. 1.
9   Hall, Michael C./Lew, Alan A. (1998, eds.): *Sustainable Tourism. A Geographical Perspective*. New York: Longman.
10   Weaver (2006): *Sustainable Tourism*.
11   Page, Stephen/Connell, Joanne (2008, eds.): *Sustainable Tourism. Critical Concepts in the Social Sciences, Vol. 1 Evolution and Context of Sustainable Tourism*. Abingdon/New York: Routledge.
12   Mowforth/Munt (2003): *Tourism and Sustainability*.
13   Wheeller, Brian (1991): *Tourism's Troubled Times. Responsible Tourism Is Not the Answer*. In: Page/Connell (2008, eds.): Sustainable Tourism, pp. 538–545.
14   Weaver (2006): *Sustainable Tourism*, p. 41.

15 Cf. Mowforth/Munt (2003): *Tourism and Sustainability,* p. 94.

16 Dernoi after Fennell, David A. (2006): *Tourism Ethics.* Clevedon/Buffalo/Toronto: Channel View Publications (Aspects of Tourism 30), p. 5.

17 Cf. Weaver (2006): *Sustainable Tourism,* p. 51.

18 Mowforth/Munt (2003): *Tourism and Sustainability,* p. 95.

19 Ibid.

20 Weaver (2006): *Sustainable Tourism,* p. 193.

21 Weaver (2006): *Sustainable Tourism.*

22 Page/Connell (2008): *General Introduction.* p. 1.

23 Hall/Lew (1998): *Sustainable Tourism.*

24 Hardy, Anne/Beeton, Robert J. S./Pearson, Leonie (2002): *Sustainable Tourism. An Overview of the Concept and its Position in Relation to Conceptualisations of Tourism.* In: Page/Connell (2008, eds.): Sustainable Tourism, pp. 416–441.

25 Page/Connell (2008): *Sustainable Tourism.*

26 Cf. Weaver (2006): *Sustainable Tourism.*

27 Page/Connell (2008): *General Introduction.* p. 1.

28 Weaver (2006): *Sustainable Tourism,* p. 12.

29 Cf. World Tourism Organization (UNWTO) (2004): *Indicators of Sustainable Development for Tourism Destinations: A Guidebook.* Madrid: UNWTO, p. 7.

30 Ibid.

31 Page/Connell (2008): *General Introduction.* p. 11.

32 Müller, Hansruedi (1994): *The Thorny Path to Sustainable Tourism Development,* In: Page/Connell (2008, eds.): Sustainable Tourism, pp. 504–511, p. 505.

33 Ibid., p. 506.

34 The Austrian Kurt Luger, e.g. names the components (1) langfristig möglich; (2) kulturell verträglich; (3) sozial ausgewogen; (4) ökologisch tragfähig; and (5) wirtschaftlich sinnvoll und ergiebig. Cf. Luger, Kurt (2007): *Auf der Suche nach dem Ort des ewigen Glücks. Kultur, Tourismus und Entwicklung im Himalaya.* Innsbruck/Wien/Bozen: Studienverlag, p. 148.

35 Ibid.

36 Mowforth/Munt (2003): *Tourism and Sustainability,* p. 99.

37 Cf. Hall/Lew (1998): *Sustainable Tourism,* p. 40.

38 Cf. ibid.

39 Cf. Weaver (2006): *Sustainable Tourism,* p. 135.

40 Cf. ibid.

41 Cf. Zimmermann, Willi (2006): *Good Governance in Destination Management.* In: Jamieson, Walter (ed.): Community Destination Management in Developing Economies. New York/London/Oxford: Haworth Hospitality Press, pp. 113–122, p. 116.

42 Cf. Mowforth/Munt (2003): *Tourism and Sustainability,* p. 215.

43 Simmons, David G. (1994): *Community participation in tourism planning.* In: Tourism Management, 15 (2), pp. 98–105.

44 Cf. Zimmermann (2006): *Good Governance in Destination Management,* p. 116.

45 In his article, Zimmermann used the word "equity". The author assumes that Zimmermann confused the similar words equity and equality. This assumption becomes plausible by returning to the original: "Equity in participation (each different group or sector should be equally represented)". Without a doubt, the definition given in brackets refers to the concept of equality. However, it cannot be clarified if Zimmermann quoted Simmons incorrectly or if already Simmons used the wrong concept.

46 Cf. ibid.

47 Cf. ibid.

48 Ibid., p 118.

49 Department for International Development (DFID) (1999): *Tourism and Poverty Elimination. Untapped Potential,* p. 1. Available from: www.haroldgoodwin.info/ppt/dfid_summary.PDF [03.01.2013].

50 Cf. Ibid., p. 6. This classification, based on the pioneering *Sustainable Tourism and Poverty Elimination Study* Bennett et al. carried out for DFID, has become widely accepted, albeit without being

updated since its publication in 1999. These days, the international poverty line, first proposed in 1990 by the World Bank for measuring absolute poverty, is subject to a broad academic and political debate since it has never been adapted to certain parameters, e.g. inflation. However, it is not the purpose of this paper to portray this discussion. For further details see e.g. Ravallion, Martin/ Chen, Shaohua/Sangraula, Prem (2009): *Dollar a Day Revisited*. In: The World Bank Economic Review, Vol. 23 (2), pp. 163–184. Available from: https://openknowledge.worldbank.org/bitstream/ handle/10986/4499/wber_23_2_163.pdf?sequence=1 [14.08.2013].

51 DFID (1999): *Tourism and Poverty Elimination*, p. 1.

52 Ibid.

53 Ashley, Caroline/Boyd, Charlotte/Goodwin, Harold (2000): *Pro-Poor Tourism. Putting Poverty at the Heart of the Tourism Agenda*. In: Natural Resource Perspectives, No. 51, p. 6. Available from: www.odi.org.uk/sites/odi.org.uk/files/odi-assets/publications-opinion-files/2861.pdf [14.08.2013].

54 Mowforth/Munt (2003): *Tourism and Sustainability*.

55 Luger (2007): *Auf der Suche nach dem Ort des ewigen Glücks*.

56 Ashley/Boyd/Goodwin (2000): *Pro-Poor Tourism*.

57 Bennett, Oliver/Roe, Dilys/Ashley, Caroline (1999): *Sustainable Tourism and Poverty Elimination Study. A Report to the Department for International Development*. Available from: www.propoor-tourism.info/documents/SustT1999.pdf [03.01.2013].

58 World Tourism Organization (UNWTO) (2002): *Tourism and Poverty Alleviation*. Madrid: UNWTO.

59 Mowforth/Munt are still using the nowadays negatively connoted term "Third World". In their opinion, the word "development" and its derivatives imply that "there is an end state to the process of development and that all countries will eventually reach a 'developed' state. By contrast, there are strong grounds for arguing that the process of development is one which actually causes under-development elsewhere […]". The term "Third World", in this case not used as synonymous for the non-aligned countries during the Cold War, however, "helps to emphasise the ways in which power, resources and development are unequally and unevenly shared globally […]". Mowforth/ Munt (2003): *Tourism and Sustainability*, p. 5.

60 Cf. Nawijn, Jeroen/Peeters, Paul/van der Sterren, Jos (2008): *The ST-EP Programme and Least Developed Countries. Is Tourism the Best Alternative?* In: Burns, Peter/Novelli, Marina (eds.): Tourism Development: Growth, Myths and Inequalities. Wallingford: CAB International; pp. 1–10, p. 2.

61 Cf. Luger, Kurt (2006): *Tourismus als Entwicklungsmodell. Nachhaltigkeitsversuche, Armutsreduzierung und Regionalentwicklung*. In: Baumhackl, Herbert/Habinger, Gabriele/Kolland, Franz/ Luger, Kurt (eds.): Tourismus in der "Dritten Welt". Zur Diskussion einer Entwicklungsperspektive. Wien: Promedia/Südwind (Historische Sozialkunde/Internationale Entwicklung 25), pp. 127–152, pp. 128–129.

62 Hunter, Colin (1997): *Sustainable Tourism as an Adaptive Paradigm*. In: Page/Connell (2008, eds.): Sustainable Tourism, pp. 442–461, p. 442.

63 Weaver (2006): *Sustainable Tourism*, p. 10.

64 Nawijn/Peeters/van der Sterren (2008): *The ST-EP Programme and Least Developed Countries*, p. 5.

65 Hall/Lew (1998): *Sustainable Tourism*, p. 23.

66 Cf. Ura, Karma (2004): *The Bhutanese Development Story*, pp. 4–5. Available from: www.bhutan-studies.org.bt/publicationFiles/Monograph/mono-1en-bt-dev-stry.pdf [20.11.2013].

67 Cf. Planning Commission/Royal Government of Bhutan (PC/RGoB) (1999): *Bhutan 2020. A Vision for Peace, Prosperity and Happiness, Part 1*. Thimphu: RGoB, p. 4. Available from: www.gnhc.gov. bt/wp-content/uploads/2011/05/Bhutan2020_1.pdf [14.11.2013].

68 Ibid., p. 6.

69 Priesner, Stefan (1999): *Gross National Happiness. Bhutan's Vision of Development and its Challenges*. In: Kinga, Sonam/Galay, Karma/Rapten, Phuntsho/Pain, Adam (eds.): Gross National Happiness: A Set of Discussion Papers, pp. 24–52, p. 24. Available from: http://www.bhutanstudies.org.bt/ publicationFiles/OccasionalPublications/GNH-SetofDiscussionPapers/GNH_Ch3_Priesner.pdf [02.11.2013].

70 Ibid, p. 26.

71 Cf. Ura (2004): *The Bhutanese Development Story*, p. 3.

72 Priesner (1999): *Gross National Happiness*, p. 27.

73 Ibid., p. 24.

74 Ibid.

75 Ura, Karma/Alkire, Sabina/Zangmo, Tshoki/Wangdi, Karma (2012): *An Extensive Analysis of GNH Index*. Thimphu: Centre for Bhutan Studies, p. 6. Available from: www.grossnationalhappiness. com/wpcontent/uploads/2012/10/An%20Extensive%20Analysis%20of%20GNH%20Index.pdf [22.12.2012].

76 Gross National Happiness Commission (GNHC)/Royal Government of Bhutan (RGoB) (2009): *Tenth Five Year Plan 2008–2013*. Vol. 1, Main Document. Thimphu: GNHC/RGoB, p. 17. Available from: www.gnhc.gov.bt/wpcontent/uploads/2011/10thplan/TenthPlan_Vol1_Web.pdf [04.12.2012].

77 Ura, Karma/Alkire, Sabina/Zangmo, Tshoki (2011): *The Gross National Happiness Index of Bhutan. Method and Illustrative Results*. Thimphu: Centre for Bhutan Studies (Powerpoint), p. 2. Available from: www.oecd.org/site/ssfc2011/48920513.pdf [23.12.2013].

78 Cf. Dorji, Kinley (2012): *Why Bhutan? A GNH Perspective*. Available from: www.kuenselonline. com/why-bhutan-a-gnh-perspective/#.UyLmx86ylbw [30.12.2012].

79 Ura et al. (2012): *An Extensive Analysis of GNH Index*, p. 7.

80 Ibid.

81 GNHC/RGoB (2009): *Tenth Five Year Plan*, p. 18.

82 Ura et al. (2012): *An Extensive Analysis of GNH Index*, p. 6.

83 GNHC/RGoB (2009): *Tenth Five Year Plan*, p. 17.

84 Cf. Dorji (2012): *Why Bhutan?*

85 Cf. Obrecht, Andreas J. (2010): *Bhutan. Königreich des Glücks?* In: Obrecht, Andreas J. (ed.): Sanfte Transformation im Königreich Bhutan. Soziokulturelle und technologische Perspektiven. Wien/ Köln/Weimar: Böhlau, pp. 15–73, p. 27.

86 Cf. Dorji (2012): *Why Bhutan?*

87 Cf. Ura et al. (2012): *An Extensive Analysis of GNH Index*.

88 To measure GNH, the Centre for Bhutan Studies and GNH Research developed the *Gross National Happiness Index* (GNH Index) for RGoB. Based on the four pillars and nine dimensions, 33 indicators and 124 variables were identified. The GNH Index methodology and the key findings of the survey conducted in 2010 can be seen in Ura et al. (2012): *An Extensive Analysis of GNH Index*. The Austrian film-maker Harald Friedl and his crew accompanied the ambitious project of measuring GNH across the country. The documentary "What Happiness is" tells this story. Friedl, Harald (2012): *What Happiness Is*. DVD. kurt mayer film.

89 Cf. GNHC/RGoB (2009): *Tenth Five Year Plan*, p. 21–22.

90 Ura (2004): *The Bhutanese Development Story*, p. 5.

91 Ibid.

92 Cf. Ibid., pp. 5–6.

93 Cf. Priesner (1999): *Gross National Happiness*, p. 30, 33.

94 Ibid.

95 Ibid., p. 35.

96 GNHC/RGoB (2009): *Tenth Five Year Plan*, p. 17.

97 Planning Commission/Royal Government of Bhutan (PC/RGoB) (1999): *Bhutan 2020. A Vision for Peace, Prosperity and Happiness. Part 2*. Thimphu: PC/RGoB, p. 7. Available from: www.gnhc. gov.bt/wp-content/uploads/2011/05/Bhutan2020_2.pdf [14.11.2013].

98 Ibid.

99 Ibid., p. 10.

100 Ibid., p. 8.

101 Cf. Dujardin, Marc (1994): *Bhutan's Human Settlements. The Dynamics of Tradition and Modernity*. In: Aris, Michael/Hutt, Michael (eds.): Bhutan. Aspects of Culture and Development. Gartmore: Kiscadale Ltd. (Kiscadale Asia Research Series 5), pp. 137–171, p. 153.

102 Cf. e.g. PC/RGoB (1999): *Bhutan 2020. Part 1*, p. 24.

103 Cf. Priesner, Stefan (2010): *Bhutans sanfte Transformation*. In: Obrecht, Andreas J. (ed.): Sanfte Transformation im Königreich Bhutan. Soziokulturelle und technologische Perspektiven. Wien/ Köln/Weimar: Böhlau, pp. 201–219, p. 214.

104 Aris, Michael/Hutt, Michael (1994, eds.): *Bhutan. Aspects of Culture and Development*. Gartmore: Kiscadale Ltd. (Kiscadale Asia Research Series 5).

105 Dujardin (1994): *Bhutan's Human Settlements*, p. 147.

106 Mathou, Thierry (1994): *The Growth of Bhutanese Diplomacy 1961–91. Opportunities and Challenges.* In: Aris/Hutt (eds.): Bhutan, pp. 51–85, p. 51.

107 Cf. Obrecht, Andreas J. (2010, ed.): *Sanfte Transformation im Königreich Bhutan*, pp. 214–215.

108 Cf. Luger (2007): *Auf der Suche nach dem Ort des ewigen Glücks*, pp. 155–161.

109 United Nations (UN) (2012): *66/281. International Day of Happiness.* Resolution adopted by the General Assembly on 28 June 2012. Available from: www.un.org/ga/search/view_doc.asp?symbol=A/RES/66/281 [29.11.2013].

110 Sachs, Jeffrey/Helliwell, John/Layard, Richard (2012, eds.): *World Happiness Report.* Available from: www.earth.columbia.edu/sitefiles/file/Sachs%20Writing/2012/World%20Happiness %20Report.pdf [07.12.2013].

111 Available from: www.newdevelopmentparadigm.bt [29.01.2014].

112 UN (2012): *66/281. International Day of Happiness.*

113 Dorji (2012): *Why Bhutan?*

114 Ibid.

115 Ibid.

116 Mathou (1994): *The Growth of Bhutanese Diplomacy,* p. 74.

117 Cf. GNHC/RGoB (2009): *Tenth Five Year Plan,* p. 35.

118 Cf. Obrecht (2010): *Bhutan. Königreich des Glücks?,* p. 40.

119 Cf. Rai, Rajesh (2013): *More Competition, Less Opportunities.* Available from: www.kuenselonline. com/more-competition-less-opportunities/#.U8Znq7EzyUk [18.08.2013].

120 Cf. Scofield, John (1974): *Bhutan Crowns a New Dragon King.* In: National Geographic Magazine, Vol. 146 (4), pp. 546–571, p. 561.

121 Cf. Mayhew, Bradley/Brown, Lindsay/Mahapatra, Anirban (2011): *Bhutan.* Singapore: Lonely Planet, p. 202.

122 Dorji, Tandi (2001): *Sustainability of Tourism in Bhutan.* In: Journal of Bhutan Studies, Vol. 3, pp. 84–104, p. 84. Available from: www.bhutanstudies.org.bt/publicationFiles/JBS/JBS_Vol3No1/3. tourism.pdf [03.05.2012].

123 Tourism Council of Bhutan (TCB) (n.d.): *About TCB.* Available from: www.tourism.gov.bt/about-tcb/about-tcb [20.12.2013].

124 GNHC/RGoB (2009): *Tenth Five Year Plan,* p. 107.

125 Cf. Ibid., p. 106.

126 Cf. Dorji (2001): *Sustainability of Tourism in Bhutan,* p. 84.

127 Ibid.

128 Cf. Planning Commission (PC) (1982): *Fifth Five Year Plan 1981–1986.* Available from: www.gnhc. gov.bt/wpcontent/uploads/2011/04/05fyp.pdf [16.12.2013].

129 It is worth mentioning that, while older documents like the 10th FYP (2009) or the Vision 2020 (1999) exclusively use the concept low volume, documents as recent as the Tourism Monitor 2012 (2013) use both concepts.

130 Cf. Planning Commission (PC) (1993): *Seventh Five Year Plan 1992–1997,* p. 2. Available from: www.gnhc.gov.bt/wp-content/uploads/2011/04/07fyp.pdf [16.12.2013].

131 Cf. Planning Commission (PC) (1998): *Eight Five Year Plan 1998–2003,* p. 187. Available from: www.gnhc.gov.bt/wpcontent/uploads/2011/04/08fyp.pdf [16.12.2013].

132 Cf. Fraser, Neil/Bhattacharya, Anima/Bhattacharya, Bimalendu (2001): *Geography of a Himalayan Kingdom: Bhutan.* New Dehli: Concept Publishing Company.

133 Cf. Ibid.

134 Dorji, Sonam, General Secretary, ABTO, *Interview,* 4 February 2013 in Thimphu, Bhutan.

135 Cf. Dorji (2001): *Sustainability of Tourism in Bhutan,* p. 84.

136 Cf. ibid., p. 85.

137 Cf. GNHC/RGoB (2009): *Tenth Five Year Plan,* p. 106.

138 Cf. ibid.

139 Tourism Council of Bhutan (TCB) (n.d.): *About TCB.* Available from: www.tourism.gov.bt/about-tcb/about-tcb [20.12.2013].

140 Cf. Association of Bhutanese Tour Operators (ABTO) (n.d.): *Home.* Available from: www.abto.org. bt [17.12.2013].

141 Cf. Hotel and Restaurant Association of Bhutan (HRAB) (n.d.): *Home*. Available from: www.hrab. org.bt [17.12.2013].

142 Cf. Guides Association of Bhutan (GAB) (n.d.): *Home*. Available from: www.gab.org.bt [17.12.2013].

143 Handicraft Association of Bhutan (HAB) (n.d.): *Home*. Available from: www.handicraftsbhutan. org [17.12.2013].

144 Since 2013, the state-owned airline Druk Air with headquarters in Paro is flanked by Bhutan's first private airline, Tashi Air Pvt. Ltd. Under the name Bhutan Airlines it is operating flights to India, Nepal and Thailand. Cf. Dorji, Gyalsten K. (2015): *Tashi Air launches New Delhi flights*. Available from: www.kuenselonline.com/tashi-air-launches-new-delhi-flights [27.09.2017]; Bhutan Airlines (n.d.): *Corporate Profile*. Available from: bhutanairlines.bt/coporateporfile [27.09.2017].

145 TCB (n.d.): *About TCB*.

146 Cf. Department of Tourism (DOT) (1999): *Rules and Regulations for Tour Operations in Bhutan*. Thimphu: DOT.

147 Ibid., p. 1, 8.

148 Cf. Tourism Council of Bhutan (TCB) (2013): *Bhutan Tourism Monitor. Annual Report 2012*. Thimphu: TCB, p. 64.

149 Tourism Council of Bhutan (TCB) (n.d.): *Tourism Policy*. Available from: www.tourism.gov.bt/ tourismpolicy/tourism-policy [20.12.2013].

150 Cf. Tourism Council of Bhutan (TCB) (n.d.): *Minimum Daily Package*. Available from: www.tourism.gov.bt/plan/minimum-daily-package [20.12.2013].
The price of the minimum daily package (per person per night) is graded as follows:
For tourists travelling in a group of three persons or more:
USD 200 in winter (December, January, February) and summer (June, July, August)
USD 250 in spring (March, April, May) and autumn (September, October, November)
For tourists travelling in a group of two: surcharge of USD 30 per person per night
For a tourist travelling individually: surcharge of USD 40 per night (TCB n.d.^d)
Further, TCB grants discounts for children, full time students and groups of eleven or more people. For more details see Tourism Council of Bhutan (TCB) (n.d.): *Discounts*. Available from: www.tourism.gov.bt/plan/discounts [20.12.2013].

151 Tourism Council of Bhutan (TCB) (n.d.): *Visa*. Available from: www.tourism.gov.bt/plan/visa [20.12.2013].

152 TCB (2013): *Bhutan Tourism Monitor*, p. 71.

153 Ibid., p. 98.

154 Ibid., p. 49.

155 Scofield, John (1974): *Bhutan Crowns a New Dragon King*. In: National Geographic Magazine, Vol. 146 (4), pp. 546–571, p. 563.

156 Weaver (2006): *Sustainable Tourism*, p. 187.

157 Fraser et al., on the contrary, assume that Bhutan sticks to the principle of exclusiveness, meaning that the country is a tourist destination which only the rich are able to afford. Cf. Fraser et al. (2001): *Geography of a Himalayan Kingdom*, p. 147. In terms of marketing, this may be equated with the concept of *demarketing*. By discouraging a certain market segment – in the case of Bhutan, mass tourism – demarketing is the "opposite of target marketing" according to Weaver (2006): *Sustainable Tourism*, p. 187; although both concepts in the end lead to the same result.

158 Cf. Tourism Council of Bhutan (TCB) (2012): *Tourism Strategy and Development Plans 2013–2018 (Draft)*, 02:05 min.

159 Cf. Tourism Council of Bhutan (TCB) (2017): *Bhutan Tourism Monitor. Annual Report 2016*. Thimphu: TCB, p. 31.

160 TCB (n.d.): *About TCB*.

161 This analysis was written before the (delayed) publication of the 11th FYP. The core objective of the 11th FYP is "Self-reliance and Inclusive Green Socio-economic Development". However, in tourism RGoB pursues the objectives of the 10th FYP: The development programs of the 11th FYP, namely *Strengthening of RITH* and *Sustainable Tourism Development* differ only slightly from those of the 10th FYP, which are *Sustainable Tourism Development Programme* and *Hotel & Tourism Management Training Institute*. Cf. Gross National Happiness Commission (GNHC) / Royal Government of Bhutan (RGoB) (2013): *Elventh Five Year Plan 2013–2018, Vol. 2 Programme Profiles*. Thimphu:

62

GNHC/RGoB, pp. 107–119. Available from: www.gnhc.gov.bt/wp-content/uploads/2011/04/11th-Plan-Vol-2.pdf [12.05.2014]. This is why the author of this paper sticks to the analysis of the 10th FYP.

162 Cf. GNHC/RGoB (2009): *Tenth Five Year Plan, Vol. 2*, p. 1.
163 GNHC/RGoB (2009): *Tenth Five Year Plan, Vol. 1*, p. 106.
164 Cf. GNHC/RGoB (2009): *Tenth Five Year Plan, Vol. 2*, pp. 377–379.
165 Data source: Based on GNHC/RGoB (2009): Tenth Five Year Plan, Vol. 1, pp. 107–109.
166 Based on the exchange rate (Nu. per USD) of 48.41 of 2009. Nation Statistics Bureau (NSB) (2013): National Accounts Statistics 2013. Thimphu: NSB, p. vii. Available from: http://www.nsb.gov.bt/publication/files/pub7mz4450wg.pdf [30.11.2013].
167 GNHC/RGoB (2009): *Tenth Five Year Plan, Vol. 2*, pp. 377–381.
168 Data source: GNHC/RGoB (2009): *Tenth Five Year Plan, Vol. 2*, p. 378, 380.
169 TCB (2012): *Tourism Strategy and Development Plans 2013–2018*, p. 4.
170 Cf. Ibid., p. 2.
171 Ibid., p. 16.
172 Cf. ibid., pp. 24–25.
173 Cf. ibid., p. 4.
174 GNHC / RGoB (2009): *Tenth Five Year Plan, Vol. 1*, pp. 107–109.
175 Cf. TCB (n.d.): *About TCB*.
176 Cf. e.g. TCB (2013): *Bhutan Tourism Monitor*, pp. 61–64.

Salomé Ritterband

Tradition Re-Interpreted – A New Generation

The Children of the Ju/'hoansi San Rehearsing Traditional Heritage in the Context of Cultural Tourism in the Tsumkwe District of Namibia

Introduction

An idyllic scenario in a remote village on the edge of the Kalahari Desert: the red sun disappears behind the horizon; small bushes are draped in black; silence spreads throughout the houses, in the distance I can hear voices and children's laughter. At six pm it gets dark – pitch-black –, and chilly. My colleague Josef Wukovits and I peek over the fence to see what people are doing in their yards: there are isolated, light-giving fireplaces and shadows of people. It is the first evening of our visit in the village of Doupos, in north-eastern Namibia. The people are quite reserved and we don't know what the Ju/'hoansi think about us. We are about to ask ourselves how we'll spend the rest of the evening, when slowly and treading lightly, ten small children approach us from behind. In a half circle they surround us and look at us expectantly. I say my name and point at myself and as a consequence everyone tells us theirs. We sit down in a circle on the sandy ground. After some moments in silence and darkness, Josef and I start to sing some European children songs that they then perfectly imitate – loudly, enthusiastically and phonetically. The older kids disappear and come back with some wood to light a fire. More and more the children take over and start singing church songs, energetically, laughing, beautifully. No adult comes near, and only later in the evening, some teenage girls join the group. Now they all together sing and rhythmically clap their hands to traditional Ju/'hoansi songs in a circle-like formation, dancing one by one in the middle of it. The smaller children are chased away if they want to join the circle with their as yet uncoordinated movements. Josef and I have become silent observers of the scene.

The Ju/'hoansi in the Tsumkwe District of the northern part of Namibia build upon their cultural heritage to offer specific tourist programmes for visitors from all over the world. The San people – the most ancient inhabitants of Southern Africa[1] – have suffered a long history of repression and marginalisation by the majority populations and the nation states themselves[2]. The Ju/'hoansi, a subgroup of the indigenous San population, have been involved in tourism since the 1980's, when a series of unfortunate incidents brought about negative impacts for the local people involved.[3] With a more sustainable and sensitive approach, the *Nyae Nyae Conservancy* (NNC) founded in 1998, wanted tourism to become a positive source for economic and social improvement.[4] Comaroff and Comaroff see the future, if not even the economic survival of certain ethnic groups, in the commodification of culture for tourism. Culture itself becomes a source of labour and an interesting resource by which to generate income. In their statements, cultural commodification does not necessarily imply the destruction of certain habits, but much more a revival, rediscovery or even creation of new traditions.[5] Rural San communities in the remote areas of northern Namibia are no exception to this global phenomenon. The well-organised *Living Museums* are part of the *Living Culture Foundation Namibia* (LCFN) and were established by the German-Namibian founder Werner Pfeifer to help the indigenous communities of the San to make a living from their *Intangible Cultural Heritage* (ICH). Based on a similar idea, *Cultural Villages* that are located inside the *Nyae Nyae Conservancy* (NNC) work with *Community Based Natural Resource Management* (CBNRM) to combine the protection of the natural environment with human development and economic benefits from tourism. In both these concepts, the people at the centre of this have worked upon their "traditional" activities in order to make them adapt them to cultural heritage programmes that can be booked for a fee by tourists. The Ju/'hoansi of these specific villages use traditional clothes and have reconstructed traditional villages with straw huts that they use as designated performance spaces. However, in ordinary life they live in "modern" villages that are located around 100 to 500 m. apart. The establishment of two different sites was originally introduced to avoid troublesome intrusion into their private lives by regular visitors.

This paper is based on the material from my Master's Thesis in Social and Cultural Anthropology at the University of Vienna (2016)[6]. The data was gathered during two fieldwork trips in 2014. In January of that year I was part of a collective field practice group under the guidance of Werner Zips and Manuela Zips-Mairitsch. Together with 20 students I visited four different *Living Museums* and *Cultural Villages*, experienced a variety of different explicit cultural performances and got to know some of their inner thoughts through narrative interviews. During the field research for my Master's Thesis in August 2014, Josef Wukovits and I decided to stay in the village Doupos, where we had established some contacts during our first trip. Against our expectations we were given the opportunity to stay in the village, where the Ju/'hoansi actually live and here we placed our tent. In contrast to the first research trip we found ourselves in the area Goffman would have defined as "backstage"[7]. We could observe how the participants lived their daily lives, and what happened when tourists were announced for a cultural activity. Because of the circumstances I had to re-consider the separation between "front- and backstage"[8] and started to focus on the new generation – the children and young adults who respond to and re-develop cultural performances.

During my first days of fieldwork, I struggled to position myself in the field and tried to get in touch with the inhabitants of Doupos. The children were very important in these first days of uncertainty, as they constantly surrounded and followed us from the beginning. They were our gatekeepers to the community and our closest contacts. With them I further learned basic words in Ju/'hoansi, as they were disciplined and relentless teachers. The children and young adults were the only people who accompanied us to the performing area. They did all the activities we had experienced with the adults, who performed in exchange for a fee during my first field trip. Imitating the performances they had observed, the children explained bush food to us and organised private singing and dancing events, laughing and experimenting. The children and teenagers who grow up in this complex and diversified context, have developed their own playful strategies to deal with cultural performances and take opportunities to rehearse their embodied and acquired knowledge. Although tourism has caused a series of lamentable impacts on different, especially indigenous societies around the world, it can also be considered as a chance to reinforce the cultural heritage of a society. In the process of cultural commodification for the purposes of tourism the Ju/'hoansi themselves very often mentioned the positive impacts it has on the younger generations who learn about ancestral culture and traditions.[9] At the same time, traditional learning has been afforded little consideration within formal schooling institutions in Namibia.[10] These separate spheres of learning lead to internal struggles for the children, who at a young age find themselves torn between two opposing approaches to education.

Throughout this paper I will focus on the Ju/'hoansi children, who consciously and subconsciously learn and deal with intangible heritage in the context of cultural tourism. I will examine the future of cultural performances that are inevitably connected to the attitude of the youngest generations towards traditional knowledge and I will describe how dealing with traditional activities on an almost daily basis has an impact on the lives of the children. In the first part I will illustrate the role of tourism for the Ju/'hoansi and the process of commodification of culture. I will then have a closer look at the strategies, the children and young adults apply while handling *Intangible Cultural Heritage* in *Living Museums* and *Cultural Villages* and discuss formal learning in contrast to traditional education. Finally, I will trace possible future developments for the San involved in tourism pursuing ecological, economic and social sustainability.

The "Experience" of Ju/'hoansi Culture

The San people of Southern Africa are one of the indigenous societies most written about in anthropology[11] and their involvement in tourism attracts people from all around the world. The Ju/'hoansi seem to realise their special status in the Namibian tourism industry and tourist guide Tsemkgao !L/ae nicknamed "Smallboy" explains, why in his opinion tourists travel from far away to visit them:

> "*Cultures are actually different and some people lost their cultures. [...] You guys have heard about us, maybe have read newspapers about us or watched*

television about us and now you have decided: 'let me see them with my own eyes so that I can have the idea!' I think that this is the reason why you come here."[12]

The "Bushmen"[13] are, together with the Himba, the most prominent indigenous representatives of cultural tourism in Namibia, as Jeremy Silvester – Coordinator of the Museums Association of Namibia (MAN) – comments:

"Cultural Villages mainly cover San and Himba, because that is what tourists want. Or what people think, tourists want, I'm not always sure it's the same thing. In the perspective of African imaginary, people expect to see huts, not zinc or bricks. That's why."[14]

The images created around the San started with the hunting expeditions of Sir Francis Galton, Charles John Andersson and others at the end of the 19th century, who reported romanticising testimony about the exceptional hunting and tracking skills of the "Bushmen".[15] After World War I, the Denver African Expedition brought home first movies about the San, who were depicted as beautiful, egalitarian, harmless and prehistoric. Those same characteristics construct the "prefabricated [...] authentic bushman"[16] and are used in tourism advertising, to create a contrasting image to the touristic self[17]. Garland and Gordon describe the position of the San in Namibia that has not changed considerably until today:

"In the context of such state-sanctioned cultural commodification, it is hardly surprising that those Namibian people labelled 'bushmen' – long fetishized in ethnographies, documentaries, novels, and blockbuster films like The Gods Must Be Crazy and A Far-Off Place – have come to feature centrally in the discourse of Namibian tourism development. Indeed, tourism around so-called 'bushman' people has arguably become the hallmark of cultural tourism in Namibia, as is evidenced by the common use of bushman-style logos by safari companies."[18]

Tourism has – apart from economic and environmental effects – resulted in series of negative social impacts on the societies that are visited – especially the "classical" anthropological sites, meaning "isolated" and indigenous people. Many nation states invest in significant infrastructure for tourism, not paying attention to the actual needs of the local population and without questioning the sometimes involuntary involvement of locals.[19] Irresponsible tourism strategies and cash flows might provoke injustices and social problems, such as dissatisfaction, prostitution, and alcohol and drugs abuse. A big and generalised fear – not only of anthropologists – but of people in general is the social and cultural change that might be brought about by the "intrusion" of outsiders and the commodification of culture[20]. The constructed images of the "threatened" and "precious" cultures are derived from stereotypes that are constructed by marketing industries and often by the state itself. These images are on the one hand based on the demands of the visitors, who on the other hand dread to experience artificially staged "pseudo-events"[21]. In this way, the decision making power may rest with the consumers – the guests, who through their gaze decide how tourism attractions should be constructed – while the hosts are often portrayed as passive actors[22]. Stronza criticises the small amount of attention that has been paid to the actual living conditions of and the direct implications for the people in the host countries that are involved in tourism[23]. Their active decision making power should include the ability to choose what they want to preserve, adapt or invent.[24]

Almost 40 years ago, in the 1980's, there were no formal institutions or controlling vehicles for tourism in north-eastern Namibia; some travellers walked unwittingly into the villages, took pictures without permission, chased children around and exploited the Ju/'hoansi and !Kung buying craft products and jewellery at unfairly low prices.[25] A further danger was, that attracted by the job opportunities, particularly poor people abandoned their homes to work in tourism locations, where the pay was poor and therefore dependency was created.[26] The new influx of cash through tourism caused disagreement and conflicts in the home villages and gender inequalities grew, since men had access to work more easily. People were divided between gratitude for having a job opportunity and dissatisfaction about the little control they had over the activities happening around them. Tourists and anthropologists walked randomly into their private spheres, sometimes asking them to do offensive work and leaving very little recompense – with the excuse that San would not know about the real value of money. Some San felt it was like being observed in a zoo, especially when they started dressing in leather clothing in front of visitors to match their expectations, or when responding to actual demands from the tourists themselves. The effect on the San was social stratification inside the communities, and further they developed a growing desire for western goods, when they became aware of the economic differences between them and the visitors. Out of that came an almost obsessive pursuit of tourist cars and the San started to develop an offering for tourists. New illnesses spread because of the increased contact with outsiders. Tobacco and alcohol – that were at first distributed by anthropologists and then became a popular gift or the object of exchanges by tourists – turned out to be a big problem. The environmental impacts included, amongst other issues, the use of too many plants and roots for craft production for tourism purposes, and animals that became aggressive because of increased safari hunting.[27]

Tourism nonetheless has the capacity to economically support indigenous communities, being used as a strategy for national economic development in the fight against poverty[28]. "Pro-poor tourism" focuses on the production of direct economic benefits for poor people; enabling access to information, strengthening cultural pride and participation in society; avoiding monoculture, over-dependence and exploitation by tourism; and further teaches the population how to manage risks along with negative social and environmental impacts[29]. What is missing in the arguments put forward by Goodwin, is the actual call for the active involvement of local people in the creation of tourism projects. According to Tomaselli, successful tourism development should include poverty reduction, rely on community-led and participatory communication strategies, use low cost and up-to-date information technology, be culturally sensitive, and further be ethically and ecologically friendly[30]. Sustainable forms of tourism ideally combine environmental conservation and human development with economic profit and are labelled "alternative tourism", "ecotourism", "community-based tourism" or "cultural tourism"[31]. Development should ideally be a starting point for empowerment, promoting the active involvement of native communities in discussions about the use of their knowledge and ideas, in order to be able to control their social, economic and political status[32].

One effective way to combine tourism business, economic profit, wildlife conservation and the active engagement of the people is *Community Based Natural Resource Management* CBNRM[33]. This programme is based on a bottom-up approach, in which the local population is involved in the decision-making process. It embraces the protection of fauna and flora by the people living in the territory, giving them the possibility to profit through activities with tourists, but demanding from the visitors a respectful approach to the nature and the hosting communities. In the 1990's the *Ju Wa Bushmen Development Foundation* under the leadership of Claire Ritchie, Megan Biesele and others, seriously started thinking about concepts of eco-tourism for the Ju/'hoansi in the Tsumkwe District, with the aim of giving the indigenous people the chance to control and regulate the flows of visiting people and at the same time creating job opportunities[34]. Tourism was at that time the third largest sector of Namibian economy[35]; in 2011 direct and indirect tourism industries accounted for around 15.7 % of the total GDP and 19.7 % of national employment[36]. Inspired by successful programmes in other parts of Africa, sustainable eco-tourism was recognised as a realistic option for Namibia[37]. The government finally had to recognise that people, especially indigenous communities, can contribute to the protection of the environment, since they possess a breadth of knowledge about the fauna and flora of the area and are motivated to care for their traditional territories[38]. The San have been part of a global discussion on the affirmation of Indigenous Peoples Rights. As is the case for so many societies around the world, the San have also been deprived of their ancestral territories and have claimed access to their lands. They had to deal with especially difficult negotiations, caused by the contrast of de jure and de facto land rights, since most of the territory did not belong to them according to national law.[39] Finally, at the *National Conference on Land Reform and the Land Question* 1991, the "ancestral" lands were supposed to be ceded back to the San population of the Tsumkwe[40]. In the end, as set down in the *Communal Land Acts*, the Ju/'Hoansi obtained the right of allocation and "traditional" authorities received "customary" and "traditional" rights to their "ancestral" lands[41]. This made it possible to establish the *Nyae Nyae Conservancy* under the Nature Conservation Amendment Act 5 of 1996 at a conference of the Ministry of Wildlife Conservation and Tourism and the local organisation *Nyae Nyae Development Farmers Cooperative* (NNFC)[42]. Specific tourism regulations were established by the members of the NNC: for example the number of tourists should be controlled and tourists should not drive off the existing tracks. Tourists should approach local people with respect, ask them before taking photographs and not force people to remove their clothes. Further, specific amounts of money shall be paid for specific activities (not alcohol as it sometimes used to be) and craft items have to be bought at a fair price; the prices for the activities were recommended by the NNC. Finally, the tour guides have to be local people.[43] Following the example of the NNC in Tsumkwe District East, community leaders of West Tsumkwe started to think about their own conservancy and in 2003 the smaller *N=a Jaqna Conservancy* was established[44].

A general positive outcome of tourism is the economic benefit for the hosting society. According to Suzman, the Ju/'hoansi of the Tsumkwe District East are far better off than the San in other parts of Southern Africa[45]. Suzman found that tourism in the Nyae Nyae area is extremely economically relevant compared to agriculture and self-subsistence, the income gained through tourism is nevertheless only one source of income[46]. CBNRM nonetheless offers a strong benefit for the population in terms of capacity-building and helping to secure land rights[47]. From the point of view of the San however, income is mainly generated through tourism activities, as I identified in several interviews. Tourism for the Ju/'hoansi of the NNC has the most immediate earning capacity, whereas other sources seem to be taken less into consideration. Xoan//a and !uu, two young ladies who live in the Cultural Village of Doupos, compare the benefits from the conservancy to the ones of tourism:

> "We only have income from tourism and the conservancy, so those two. Because the income we receive from conservancy is only when the year is over. Conservancy is paying for us, a little. Each village in the conservancy is happy here, but for the basis it's tourism."[48]

The idea for the project of the LCFN instead came from Werner Pfeifer's experience up to the present day performing every summer as a caveman and Viking in Northern Germany. When he came back to Namibia – his homeland – he felt inspired to pursue his passion and relied on the cultural diversity he found here; the Ju/'hoansi especially fascinated him, and reawakened his feelings of childhood adventure.[49] In 2004 the first *Living Museum of the Ju/'hoansi-San* was founded in Grashoek, located in the *N=a Jaqna Conservancy* and in 2010 the second one followed, called *Little Hunter's Museum* and situated in the *Nyae Nyae Conservancy*. A practical reason for creating the *Living Museums* was also to avoid unwanted visitors in the private lives of the indigenous people[50]. The interest of the tourists is however sometimes limited to the wish to experience 'traditional' activities, as a guide from the Little Hunter's Museum told us about their interests:

> "Some they are interested in going to the modern villages. But many of them are interested in the traditional culture. When they come, they want to see hunting. Or they want to see people dancing and see people doing traditional things."[51]

Cultural tourism is based on the concepts of "otherness, and the discovery of the unusual and exotic, through adventure"[52], relies on the interest of the tourist in "authenticity"[53] and is structured by the "romantic gaze" of travellers[54]. Cultural tourism includes the creation of purpose-built attractions, the "preservation" of heritage, history and "tradition" and the marketing of experiences that are often claimed to be "authentic".[55] Its basis is "culture" which in this context serves as "[...] a resource, a product, an experience and an outcome"[56]. One form of cultural tourism is "indigenous tourism" that describes programmes for tourists in which indigenous culture is at the core of the offer for tourists, or when the project is managed by indigenous peoples themselves[57]. In this case, indigeneity is not seen as an inherent feature of a specific group, but as an attitude strategically constructed for specific purposes by the people who describe themselves as indigenous. Indigeneity is connected to genealogical ideas of people "from the past", but is used as an entirely modern concept for the purpose of touristic marketability. It is often at the basis for land claims and legal self-determination.[58] One of the goals of the United Nations Declaration on the Rights of Indigenous Peoples (2006) is the protection of cultural identity and indigenous heritage.[59]

It is important to include the indigenous people in the management of a project, and decision-making for example includes choices on the topic and style of presentation, as well as the images transported.[60] The imagery used within cultural tourism among the San has to be edited. Smallboy – as a tourism expert of the Tsumkwe Area East – explained in an interview, it is relevant to explain to the touring visitors how the San live when they are not performing for tourists. The LCFN focuses mainly on the "preservation of traditional culture [and the] creation of a cultural and intercultural exchange"[61] and it does so by focusing on "authentic" tools and representations. Although the cultural activities they propose to tourists are explicitly marked as part of museum activities and not as a depiction of their actual lives,[62] the revision of transported images and stereotypes is not a priority of the foundation. It was very interesting to carry out an interview with Dr. Michael Uusiku Akuupa, Namibian anthropologist and specialist on cultural festivals in his country. He advocates a national identity that in his opinion is clearly missing. Namibia is associated with some stereotypes that are commonly used on the whole African continent: pristine images of indigenous people such as the Himba or the San that because of the tourism industry are associated with the whole nation. It is common that in tourism one group becomes representative for a whole nation[63] and at the same time the indigenous groups are clustered from various ethnicities into one community that stands in contrast to "the others" inside the nation state or from other countries[64]. In Dr. Akuupa's opinion many of the stereotypes created around the San are provoked by the projects of the *Living Culture Foundation Namibia*:

"[...] the government supports those programmes that enable to create wealth through tourism. That will be one of the points on the agenda of tourists that come to Africa. But they haven't done sufficient homework to see what images are projected out to the tourists. We should have a Namibian identity, which identity is it, that we want to portray to the outside?"[65]

In my opinion both projects help to give a voice to the Ju/'hoansi by giving them the opportunity to manage and influence the images transported themselves. Although the first impression of re-enactment villages awakens associations with 18th century *Völkerschauen* or modern Disneyland-settings, the difference lies in the messages and modes of presentation. Whilst for a long time San communities were exposed or seen as "primitives", today they inform interested visitors about their culture, transmitting it as valuable knowledge and a medium of empowerment and not as an exotic characteristic. Although I concluded, that the San in *Living Museums* and *Cultural Villages* are aware of their prominence and are active stakeholders in the creation of their cultural offering for tourists, I am not so sure that this notion is grasped by all the visitors. There is still much to do to revise the images that have been loaded with stereotypes in the course of the last centuries. With the right approach indigenous tourism might indeed become a possibility for economic, political and cultural empowerment for the people who actively want to shape their identity inside the tourism industry.

Heritage Museum: A Place for Learning

I have used the term "culture" very often in the preceding chapters; as a strategy to generate income, as a controversial issue in the commodification of heritage for the purposes of tourism and as an important matter for the San in general. Its definition has been the subject of a discussion both within academia and outside that has lasted for the best part of a century, and the answer remains a complex discussion. The relevant aspect of "culture" for the purpose of this research is its connection to property and marketability. Layton and Wallace ask the question whether culture can be a commodity that can be sold[66]. It has been claimed that cultural identity is intangible and can therefore not be marketed, refusing to see the connection between economy and culture[67]. The Comaroffs challenge Bourdieu's differentiation between cultural and economic capital, claiming that in the course of cultural commodification they merge[68].

For the purpose of this research I am interested in analysing what culture means to the people who are themselves the subject of the research. "Culture" for the Ju'hoansi of the Tsumkwe is a matter related to traditional knowledge and their past. They often associate it with hunting and gathering activities, the religion of their forefathers, traditional clothing and the content of performances for tourists.[69] According to the interviews, a central issue is to keep the Ju/'hoansi culture alive and to pass on cultural knowledge to the next generation.[70] For the future, it is essential to have the new generations learning about the traditions of the San. It is important as a basis for economic security, as well as for the "preservation" of relevant knowledge and cultural identity in general. Henry / ui Nyani (guide at the *Living Museum in Grashoek* and one of the most eloquent people we met in the course of our field practice) explained in several ways what "culture" means to him:

"Culture is the meaning, that you are the person who stays in the bush. You know exactly how to stay there, to survive in the field. [...] Culture is the history. The history about the old things, and the things which we are teaching the children."[71]

Museums are one aspect of Namibia's attempt to reinforce development and cultural safeguarding through cultural tourism. The exhibition of traditional objects in museums was however an inadequate representation of Namibia's *Intangible Cultural Heritage* (ICH). The idea of museums as areas of exhibition, showing a static and objectified approach to culture, was brought to Namibia by European travellers[72]. The Namibian strategy to accomplish the aims set down in the UNESCO convention, was initially to host cultural festivals for traditional dances and music. Subsequently, *Cultural Villages* were identified as a fruitful strategy for the purpose of using ICH in terms of living practices, and to combine it with economic benefits from cultural tourism for indigenous communities in Namibia.[73] The *Museums Association of Namibia* (MAN) is the representative vehicle for all Namibian museums and heritage institutions. One important aim is to develop the cultural museum landscape for international and national tourism but at the same time they want to break from the idea of museums as exclusively tourist attractions. In their opinion, they should rather be the basis of promoting intra-national education and intercultural exchange:

"We are trying to get a connection with tourism. [...] The problem in Namibia is that museums are seen as something for tourists that come from far. And actually in our country we have so much of cultural diversity, environmental differences. [...] We would like to get a big come together of tourism and museums. But we haven't managed yet. Because of the ministries, we operate in different boxes. So culture and museums are under Youth, Sports and Culture, and Tourism is with Environment. That's why there is a big focus on environment and culture is neglected. One of our challenges, what makes Namibia unique, is not just the environment. In fact, environment is shaped by culture, and vice versa so these things really must be seen together. And education is again in another ministry but we think that our museums, our living museums should be seen as an asset for young Namibians, not just people flying in. So we are trying to build bridges, make links between education, tourism and cultural heritage."[74]

According to Sebastian Dürrschmidt, the culture of the Ju/'hoansi is no longer existent in the way it used to be.[75] Therefore, the *Living Museums* are a way to keep traditional knowledge "alive" and to promote cultural exchange with international visitors, between ethnic groups inside Namibia, and in national education.[76] For that reason, the LCFN has recently joined MAN, to focus more explicitly on the transmission of knowledge inside the country. These processes further aim to raise the cultural self-confidence of the Ju/'hoansi San. The LCFN describes their concept as follows:

"A Living Museum is an authentic way of presenting traditional culture. A Living Museums is a cultural school for tradition and a communal Namibian tourism business at the same time. Travelers can visit a Living Museum and thus can actively contribute to the preservation of traditional culture and fight against poverty in Namibia."[77]

Many Ju/'hoansi see the positive effect of cultural tourism not only in the teaching to outsiders, but also in the preservation and transmission of cultural heritage to the next generation. According to the LCFN and MAN, the future aim of heritage museums should also include the transmission of culture to internal school groups of Namibia. Nevertheless, it is also very important to pass on traditional knowledge to their own children. The *Living Museums* give the children the opportunity to get in touch with their roots and at the same time allow other children within the nation state to get to know the San culture:

"And I think that this project is the best project. Because now we are teaching our young children how our old life was. Because now we are not hunting anymore. Yeah, sometimes we collect our bushfood. We go out in the bush and collect bushfood. But our young children they did not see anything about hunting and do nothing. And I think this project is the best project to help our children that they must remember where they come from. And also this project is like school. Like some children from far places like Grootfontein or Ottawi or Windhoek, they come to see this life. And we are also teaching them our skills and all this kind of things."[78]

The children of the Ju/'hoansi who do not grow up in the context of cultural tourism, are more likely to forget about their ancestral traditions, and moreover the knowledge acquired in the context of cultural performances can be an important addition to formal schooling:

"I think, it is a good thing. In order for our children not to forget our culture. I have been visiting many places and most of the people there forget their culture, so I think it's a good idea to have the culture alive like here […]. It is also a part of education. Most of the people here don't know anymore how their parents were living. I think they know, but they forget because they don't practice. The idea of this project is to show how our parents were living in the past. The children have to go to school now but if the school goes out, they still have the chance to go to the Living Museum to learn something."[79]

Cultural knowledge is the result of a lifelong learning process and is embodied through experienced elders. Even though traditional activities are not practised for survival any more or on a daily basis, they persist in ordinary life and are regularly practised for purposes of tourism. These skills have been learned from their parents and grandparents. The body serves, according to Diane Taylor as a storage of memory and history from where ICH can easily be transmitted to other bodies by performance[80]. A double process took and still takes place in *Cultural Villages* and *Living Museums* – traditional knowledge was and is subconsciously incorporated during each performance (for tourists) and is at the same time combined with active research among the elders, who verbally transmit information about their heritage. Since the old generation is slowly passing away, the current generation in charge is keen to practice the traditional dances and songs. Some traditions were only passed on verbally and not physically, which is a clear loss for the actors of today – as Tsemkgao Daqm explained to us:

"I think there are a lot of things missing. Some older people know everything well and they passed away. So, there are a couple of things missing now. […] There were some older people who could tell the things in stories but they could not show or dramatize it. That is why we really don't know. We know by their stories that in the past things were like this, like this and this. But, we did not see how they were doing it."[81]

The training phase, one of seven stages of a performance described by Schechner, includes the learning of specific technical, symbolical and practical skills.[82] In every-day-life-performances as well as in the context of heritage performances, it includes the transmission and constant learning of subconsciously embodied knowledge.[83] In the case of the Ju/'hoansi the training includes life-long learning to obtain knowledge about plants, roots and hunting techniques as well as the embodiment of songs and dances. I have already claimed that a very important motivation and positive aspect of the *Living Museums* and *Cultural Villages* from the perspective of the Ju/'hoansi themselves is the transmission of knowledge to a younger generation. Movements, gestures and behaviours are incorporated through observation and repetition.[84] The children observe and participate in the activities for tourists and in doing so automatically learn the songs, listen to explanations and embody the traditional dances.

Observing, Embodying and Playing Cultural Heritage

In the village of Doupos daily activities such as cooking, washing, and producing craft items are a central part of their daily lives and are part of a routine. The activities for tourists are held outside the villages and interrupt daily work and ordinary tasks. When tourists arrived, the news would immediately spread throughout the village and make everyone drop their daily activities, jump into traditional attire and sometimes walk, sometimes run, into the traditional village and performance area. These isolated events presented a frequent, although not so predictable activity, because people were often informed by mobile phone at the last minute. The dichotomy between cultural performances and everyday life is constantly challenged by the presence of the children. They spent most part of the day playing in the village and the nearby bush, with nobody actively looking for them or asking where they were. They themselves decided what to do next or if they would pay us a visit. With us, the children spontaneously and regularly decided to stage specific performances, practicing the staged acts they regularly observed and attended with their parents. During the three weeks Josef Wukovits and I spent in Doupos, the children never went to the traditional performance area with the adults, apparently preferring to spend their time with us in the backstage and staging "as if performances"[85]. The adults of the Ju/'hoansi did not want us to go with them to the "traditional village" without formal permission from the tourist organisation. Since it became more interesting to observe the processes we had experienced from a tourist-like perspective on our previous visit from a different angle, in the end we never set one foot into the area of performance for tourists with the adults. Eventually the adults voluntarily offered to show us some activities in the "modern" village and without costumes. Instead, the children regularly accompanied us to the "traditional village" using it as the adequate staging for their imitation of the performances for tourists.

One important element of performance as well as of tourism is the aspect of play. For Lewis[86] play is one of the most important activities children engage in to learn social organisation in everyday life and to develop their "habitus"[87] by experimenting with role plays. Play is an experience and has the ability to lead people into a second reality different from ordinary life that may transport or even transform the players.[88] The aspect of learning through play is connected to the transmission of heritage and cultural knowledge to the young generation. Schechner compares children playing to the training phase in performance, in which social and technical skills are practiced without necessary formalised verbal teaching[89]. Children's learning processes are often embedded in systems that are not necessarily organised for explicit teaching; in these cases children take an active part in developing strategies to pursue their own educational process, especially following relatives and members of society in their daily lives.[90] The most simple, universal and sometimes the primary strategy for learning is observing, without explicit verbal instruction being needed.[91] A child imitates people's actions and learns by practicing – where a scholarly institution is absent the whole society works as knowledge transmitting network.[92] Children practice and interpret in play what they observe and imitate in ordinary life – an important occasion to embody culturally relevant behaviours and actions.[93] The embodiment of social behaviour and cultural patterns is essential for children's development and acquisition of social skills,[94] since each person moves through society and relates to others with a specific "habitus"[95].

"Yes, when she is dancing with the men, she used to always tell the kids 'you see, you must always go with the men if they are singing and dancing. You also have to dance. Don't just sing'"[96], explains N!ae Komtsa from the *Little Hunter's Museum*.

During the official activities for tourists, the youngest often formed their own dance circle next to the adults. The children enthusiastically danced all evening long, despite being chased away regularly by the grown-ups. The learning of the dances and songs needed for the shows mostly happens in an experiential manner, by following the experienced adults in their dancing and not explicitly practicing specific postures and movements[97]. Dances are part of the everyday-life and constantly experienced, children participate and imitate them, even simulating falling into a trance seen in the *Healing Dances*[98]. The children and adolescents have always been involved in the dances and trained to learn and embody their cultural heritage – this might not be a new development but through the possibility of economic benefit by being a performing participant in a *Healing Dance* – not only as a healer – the motivation to learn the songs and dances grows. Twice the children were themselves the protagonists of dances performed exclusively for us. In the introduction I described the first evening I spent in Doupos. Another day, on one of our playing tours with the children, they led us to the "traditional village", where they pulled out a drum from a hut and started to play, sing and dance. To our eyes it seemed incredibly professional and fluent: the children sang with loud voices and danced complicated moves. Their dance rhythm was much faster, livelier and playful than the songs we had heard by the adult performers.

In the course of an interview we asked Tsemkgao Daqm about learning during a performance and he explained that not only do children have to learn, but rather all adults equally.[99] The knowledge about traditional activities is a prerequisite for being able to participate in cultural performances. Since the body is carrier of cultural patterns in Bourdieu's sense of the habitus, intangible performances such as dances can be stored and transmitted as a repertoire by the body[100]. In Schechner's theory a good performance means that a role has been successfully incorporated by the individual[101]. Through repetitions, practice is incorporated and becomes part of personal embodied behaviours[102]. The "hexis" as a pattern of postures linked to a series of bodily techniques can, according to Bourdieu, be transmitted to children by the adults of society through observation and the repeated imitation of gestures, postures, expressions and ways of walking and talking[103]. In *Living Museums* some of the performance knowledge has to be explicitly learned and practiced. Indeed, during the dancing activities for tourists, I could see that the quality of the movements differed considerably between the dancers:

> *"Me I am not a dancer…* [laughs]*…and also the other ones they are just learning…that is why they dance.* […] *Yeah just learn from the other ones and that ones who are dancing the elephant dance don't know how to dance the giraffe dances. That is why you see only the young boys, young men they are the ones who are dancing the giraffe and as they are singing the elephant song, the head man, he comes to dance because he knows that the other ones, that the young men, they don't know very well how to dance the elephant dance."*[104]

On our second morning, while I was in the village craft making, Josef went out running in the bush, when a group of around ten children excitedly followed him. What he experienced was a shortened "Action Day" as offered on the official activities list that contains a *Bushwalk* as well as "traditional" singing acts. On their way through the bush, the children formed a row, attentively making sure that Josef did not get stuck in bushes or trip over on rocks and explained to him about many plants in a language he could not understand. In contrast to the ones organised by the adults, the young boys climbed up the trees to pick some fruit that Josef could taste. Alone with an adult visitor, the children seriously and professionally imitated the guided tours undertaken by their parents, discussing amongst each other and giving long explanations in Ju/'hoansi. Whilst some technical skills and routines were not yet embodied, the knowledge about roots and plants was definitely present.

On our fourth day in Doupos – when Josef and I made our daily visit to the neighbour's yard, greeting *"X!aisi!"*[105] and joining them for tea – the people suddenly started laughing and joking with us and then proceeded to dress us up in their traditional garments, which they had collected from different households. I did not really understand, but I Imaged out that something was going to happen. Between a lot of chatting and some photo-sessions, we realised that the two young men, Kha//ha and !Kunta =Oma, who had not participated in the tourism activities over recent days, would now take us on a *Bushwalk* and *Hunting Trip*. The elders did not come with us and instructed the youngsters on how to carry out the upcoming activity. The boys were dressed traditionally, although !Kunta kept his neon coloured green-orange underpants that were visible underneath his *tjona*[106]. Parodying the explanations given during the commodified tours of the adults, making a lot of jokes and with explicit "make-believe"-plays, for two and a half hours, the teenagers led us through the bush. It was a very relaxed trip, with a lot of joking and chatting and even after we asked them a couple of times, they did not want money. Josef and I had to adopt "traditional" gender roles, playing a stereotyped San man or San woman with their specific tasks. Josef had the role of an expert hunter – he had to guide the two young boys on the hunt for a duiker[107]. The boys had to show Josef explicitly how to move, since he did not have the right embodied hunting postures, for example crawling on the earth without making any noise, and running quickly when an animal was sighted. Of course, there was not even the shadow of an animal, but Josef was jokingly blamed, if he let go of the chase. I played the role of a young San woman and gatherer who should learn her tasks to be able to marry a good hunter. I was told to dig out a wateroot, which actually was not a real one, as they told us silently. I was not very elegant and successful in doing this, but it was clearly visible that the two young men were not either. When they finally had dug out the wateroot – which in contrast to the experienced hunters in the *Living Museum of Grashoek* they did with much less body effort – !Kunta showed us – like the adults normally did – how to drink the water pressed out of the root. He did not however drink it for real, instead he let the liquid flow beside his mouth. During our break I was told to make a fire (to be qualified for marriage) and even though I tried hard, I did not succeed. So Kha//ha and !Kunta tried too, but they were no more successful. When clever and naughty !Kunta realised that Josef – now in his role of a tourist – was filming, he thought of a solution and picked out some matchsticks he found in his traditional leather bag. With a quick gesture, while I was turning the fire stick, he lit the dry grass. After failing to make a good bird trap with a greenish and irregular rope knotted around some unevenly disposed sticks !Kunta performed the known "bird trap act". I had experienced this imitation of a bird falling into a self-made trap with the adults some months ago and he had evidently embodied it perfectly. As a gatherer lady I was summoned to free the bird and put it into the bag, so I became part of the "real performance" remaining in my officially assigned though unrehearsed role.[108]

When we stayed at the "modern village" of Doupos, the pre-school children were themselves the driving force of *Bushwalks, Hunting Trips* and singing evenings they organised for us. They actively used us to put the things they had learned at the cultural performances from the adults into practice. Playing in the village or going to the traditional village they imitated the activities, laughing, experimenting, but at the same time with a professional attitude.

Learning for the Future

During the first field practice I observed that the children and young people always followed their parents on performed traditional activities and participated in singing and dancing afternoons: from small babies bound on the backs of their mothers, to small children playfully imitating the dance circles, up to teenagers assuming more important tasks during the performances. The second time I undertook field research, when I remained in the backstage area, we happened to be "practice tourists" for the younger generation training their cultural knowledge. Observing their parents and growing up in this special context, the children seemed to subconsciously incorporate dance movements and specific songs in a very playful manner. The young adults and older teenagers, did not participate in the traditional activities for tourists in their daily lives, but loved to parody the things they saw their parents do, for us – anthropologists and visitors. Actively trying to apply what they have seen and learned, the smaller children showed the interest of the youngest generation to actually deal with their cultural heritage in an subconscious and playful way. San children especially learn by observing and following, as Bruce Parcher – American teacher adviser of the "San Education Project"[109] in Tsumkwe – has recognised:

> "That is, yeah it's oral, but it's also through trial and error, through play, through observation. San kids learn mostly through observation, just watching and following their parents around. And then playing and doing."[110]

Observation is at the core of unofficial learning strategies, by following the parents doing common activities, and by practicing and imitating[111]. Playing is another fundamental aspect of learning, in which techniques are exercised and embodied, that might later serve a purpose in daily life in a society[112]. Margaret Mead further recognised the centrality of role play for children's acquisition of social skills and their learning process[113]. According to Gray who studied "hunters and gatherers societies", parents do not have specific strategies to educate their children but rely on playful and experimental approaches to rehearse the skills and ideas of their culture[114]. San children constantly follow and observe their parents, they practice in play until it gradually grows into "real" activity[115]. Play is a central activity of children universally and stands in contrast to formalised education, where an authority in a hierarchical system transmits specific knowledge to its pupils[116].

Education and schooling is a big problem in the Nyae Nyae area, since the schooling system is not compatible with San children's situation[117]. A high drop-out rate is prevalent for San school children because they fear school, are often treated badly by the majority population teachers and pupils, and are often bullied because of their poor clothing by other kids. This again leads to poor job opportunities and a marginal position within society[118]. Only one in five children attends school and only 1% of the San are able to continue up to senior secondary education level[119]. The further away the schools are geographically from the traditional communities, the more difficult it is for the San children to reach them – as Bruce Parcher explained us: *"Some tried and the dropout rate is exceedingly high for the kids in this area: 95–100%. Most of them drop out when they have to come to Tsumkwe."*[120]

The schooling approach of formalised knowledge and the education used to pass down cultural heritage are poles apart. For Memory Simasiku, a teacher at Grashoek primary school, these are two different areas in which parents and schools have to work together to educate the children in both categories[121]. Bruce Parcher confirms that the parent's contribution is essential for his school projects, in which he tries to involve cultural knowledge and mother tongue language into the school programme[122].

> *"It is definitely education. It's the kind of thing that we as teachers would not be able to teach them. Let me say it's another part of education in a child's life. As a pre-primary teacher, we are taught to teach the child in a whole, not just in one subject, but the whole child entirely. When they teach the children how to do something at home, us, the teachers are working on a child's mind. Also the parents are working on a child's mind at home, preparing them for the future, for instance. You know, most of the people here drop out of the school, and what they are taught at home is what keeps them going, keeps them further. For instance, if the child drops out of school for a reason, any reason, they still have what they learned at home."*[123]

In the eyes of another primary school teacher in Grashoek, a Kavango woman called Perpetwa Hausiku, the *Living Museums* are an extremely good project for the children. They provide a cultural school for the younger generations, where they get curious about their heritage simply because they are surrounded by it and start observing and asking questions: *"Yeah, the kids love it. They love practicing their culture. A lot."*[124]

On the one hand, schooling may sometimes get in the way of children's' dealing with "traditional" heritage. I observed in Doupos, that there were few children aged seven to sixteen because most of them were living with their relatives in Tsumkwe and were busy at school. It kept them very occupied and even for children who lived in Doupos or came back for holidays, there was little time to show interest in the traditional activities or to follow their parents lead. Koba, a beautiful and smart young lady aged eight who lived in Doupos, is a great singer and dancer but when I chatted with her, she told me that she could not go to the museum area with her parents because of school; she only went there to play in her free time. I also met

Cwi, who was always perfectly dressed in modern clothes and spoke perfect English. He was very ambitious and the only teenager I met who enthusiastically went to school and was about to finish. He wanted to become a pilot and go to school in Grootfontein or Windhoek and he laughingly told me, with a touch of superiority, that the cultural activities did not interest him, he had no time for that. As a school teacher, Perpetwa Hausiku has a good insight into these dynamics:

> "The parents felt that the kids are kept most of the time in school and after the school, let me put it his way, most of the parents are out practicing or performing and dancing at the campsite, so they don't have enough time to teach their kids some of their practices."[125]

On the other hand, traditional activities may also come into conflict with school attendance, leading to a vicious circle. Although parents absolutely motivate their children to get an education, Ju/'hoansi children are raised very independently and are free to make their own decisions[126]. Since the San children's situation in public schools is very poor and cultural activities are a realistic alternative for the future, some children and teenagers prefer to stay at home, as Bruce critically commented:

> "Because of the dropout rates and the choice that kids make in the San culture, the kids can choose whether to go to school or not. The choice some kids make, is to stay and live a traditional life in the village and not go to school. But the parents, I've never heard a single parent say they don't support education. They all want their kids to go to school, they just don't want it to be like it is now. […] One of the interesting things, those kids are very in touch with their culture, very proud to be Ju/'hoansi and that makes it harder for them to come here. So they all dropped out last year. They really…because of this, the village is quite successful because of the Living Museum and the parents attitudes to education is very strong they want their kids to go school. So there's a lot of push from both sides."[127]

The *Living Museums* and *Cultural Villages* are optimal job opportunities for the future, as Memory Simasiku observed in Grashoek:

> "The Living Museum is an important source of income here. It is the only source of income. So inevitably they teach their children about their culture, even though they might teach them in the sense 'It's going to be your job. It's going to be your future job'."[128]

For the new generation of young adults and teenagers, the occupation with traditional heritage becomes even more interesting. Whereas Dabe and Cwi //ao, 18 and 22 years old, gave up performing as well as schooling to take up regular jobs at the conservancy, others wished to learn more about the performances. Although in the case of 16 years old !Kunta the interest in learning was smaller, but instead the desire to show off in front of us seemed to be more relevant, K//akha and Xoan//a showed a deeper motivation to follow their parents. It gives them the opportunity for a more or less steady income, whilst still staying in their village – a place most young people seemed quite attached to.

> "Yeah, I want them to learn the same as I learned, because when I went to school I did not know how my parents lived, then after I just grew up until 19 years and then I started to learn about gathering and hunting. And nowadays while they are still young I want them to learn these things already before they go to school and as they are at school they know already how to hunt and gather bush food, how to make arrows, clothes and so on. Because I want them, even if they finish school and have jobs, they have to think back and, the modern things, they must bring them back into the village, stay in the village, not that they decide to go away and not come back into the village. [...] It is a good idea to have this museum and to show people how our parents were living and also our youngest can learn a lot from it."[129]

Tsumkwe was a place that people of all generations visited frequently to buy things or to consume alcohol. At the same time many people, especially the young ones, complained about the noise in Tsumkwe and the bad atmosphere. Kha//ha and !Kunta regularly accentuated their desire to stay in Doupos in the future. From my very subjective perspective, some people in Tsumkwe and in other villages seemed worse off than in Grashoek or Doupos, where at least an income was guaranteed, a fact that Bruce Parcher can confirm: "Competition and jealousy and the tourists are channelled by the conservancy to certain villages, so that there is a tension between the villages included in the conservancy and the villages that are not."[130]

The future developments in cultural tourism lie in the hands of the new generation, who have embodied some of the acts and continue to develop the performances. The children, who grow up with the regular enactment of tradition, found creative and experimenting ways of learning, parodying and developing the performance of preserved and at the same time transformed "culture".

Conclusion and Prospects

Tourism has become one of the most fruitful economic sectors worldwide and its implications therefore have to be considered by anthropologists as well as by others. Alternative forms of tourism involvement may allow indigenous people to profit economically and at the same time influence the images that are transported in the course of the marketing process. By claiming rights of "customary" use of their ancestral lands, the San were able to build the Nyae Nyae Conservancy and use their natural resources and cultural heritage in a sustainable and profitable way. This development has been a starting point for the construction of an image as empowered individuals, using cultural heritage not as a basis for stereotypes but as a statement of their own expertise. Through Community Based Natural Resource

Management, local people are actively involved in the development of tourism businesses, to ensure that they profit best from them, and in doing so work towards the conservation of wildlife. Although tourism is statistically not the majority of their income – which is covered by the state and the conservancy – for the Ju/'hoansi involved, it is considered as an important factor of financial security. The main motivations to participate in cultural performances for tourists are the prospects of financial gain, an occupation and pride in their own cultural heritage, and the wish to keep it alive to transmit it to their children. There is a certain awareness that visitors from around the world take an interest in their culture and want to learn about it. The knowledge about traditional activities is a therefore a relevant premise to be able to participate in cultural performances and is acquired in a life-long process. It is partly learned through the observation and practice of participating in traditional activities – with or without tourists. *Intangible Cultural Heritage* is stored in their bodies and carried out in the course of performances[131]. Some adults nevertheless had to re-learn the movements of some activities listening to the stories of the elders and practicing to incorporate the movements until they became second nature.

The children are constantly surrounded by traditional activities and the interest to learn and to apply the *Intangible Cultural Heritage* grows. In the second field research, the only people I went to the performing area with, were children and young adults. With them, I experienced all kind of activities that I knew from my previous visits to the San and had attended in exchange for a fee. Laughing and experimenting, they presented us *Bushwalks, Hunting Trips* and singing activities. Two young men, Kha//ha and !Kunta =Oma, who usually do not participate in the activities for tourists, took me and my colleague on a *Bushwalk*, imitating the explanations given during the commodified tours and often failing, when trying to do the tricks they had seen do their parents. Only some acts, as the one I will give the name of "bird trap", was perfectly embodied and performed without mistakes. Reinterpreting, rehearsing and parodying the performances of the professional actors, the young generation loved to show us – the anthropologists – the same activities they had observed among the adults in their free time. The "habitus" is incorporated by children through observation, imitation and practice until a series of structured patterns are embodied and can consequently be applied in the varied performances of each individual[132]. During my field research I observed the development of a new style of performance – the parody, performed by the potential "actors-to-be". On the basis of their own cultural heritage, children, teens and young adults re-interpret it, practice it and play with it.

The children grow up with traditional activities in a playful manner, although the young adults might have a clearer motivation for learning: the knowledge is the basis for a job and financial security and allows them to remain in their familiar environment. It is still the case that traditional education stands in contrast to formal school instruction and therefore the new generations often feel they have to choose between both. Rarely are these two sectors connected and in some cases, the possibility to generate income through learning traditional heritage, keeps the youngsters away from schooling – which is in any case quite difficult for San children to attend because of several reasons. For successful tourism operations, specific training would however be relevant and could become an important approach to integrate Ju/'hoansi communities more effectively into setting up businesses. Indigenous communities involved in tourism tend to develop into business corporations according to Comaroff and Comaroff[133]. The more knowledge about tourism and management the hosts get, the better they can adapt to the wishes of modern tourists, without vulnerably putting themselves into risk, but instead aiming for empowerment and acceptance in the tourism industry as well as inside the national state.[134] Tsemkgao !L/ae or Smallboy – tour guide for the NNC – is a good example of the aim of professionalizing and educating people to become experts in the tourism industry. He wants to study languages and engage in further education on becoming a tour guide[135]. Education and training are an essential aspect of successful tourism operations, since the actors can actively deal with them and are not passively carried along[136]. Tourism can be a chance for the youngest generations to combine education and formal instruction with traditional heritage, using knowledge to become more professional tourism workers and one day have access to better income. Recognising the possibilities of cultural tourism could motivate them to focus on more sustainable education for the youngest generations in order to profit best from the situation. The learning of traditions and cultural values is as important as learning about how to deal with small-scale business corporations and how to deal with tourist agents as well as with the tourists themselves. I could therefore imagine, that a possible future for the cultural performances might be a move towards professionalization and more intense commercialisation of their cultural resources. This leads to a creative re-interpretation and packaging of traditional activities that are re-constructed in order to transmit knowledge to visitors. The examples of the *Living Museums* and *Cultural Villages* in north-eastern Namibia have shown that they have a precious effect on the young generation motivated to learn about their traditions – is this due to the playful approach of pre-school kids or because of the economic interests of young adults. Although the actual financial benefits of tourism operations are not yet sufficient to guarantee a stable future in the Tsumkwe area, it still motivates the young generations to actively use "culture" as a serious resource and as a basis for further development.

Notes

1   Cf. Suzman, James (2001): *An Assessment of the Status of the San in Namibia.* Windhoek: Legal Assistance Centre. Report No. 4 of 5, p. 2. Available from: http://www.lac.org.na/projects/lead/Pdf/sannami.pdf [25.03.2016].

2   Cf. Zips-Mairitsch, Manuela (2009): *Lost Lands? (Land) Rights of the San in Botswana and the Legal Concept of Indigeneity in Africa.* Berlin/Zürich: Lit Verlag.

3   Cf. Biesele, Megan/Hitchcock, Robert K. (2011): *The Ju/'hoan San of Nyae Nyae and Namibian Independence: Development, Democracy, and Indigenous Voices in Southern Africa.* US: Berghahn Books, p. 101.

4   Cf. ibid., p. 198.

5   Cf. Comaroff, Jean/Comaroff, John (2009): *Ethnicity, Inc.* Chicago/London: The University of Chicago Press, p. 3.

6 Parts of this text have also been published by the same author in the book: Ritterband, Salomé (2018): *Tracking Indigenous Heritage. Ju/'Hoansi San Learning, Interpreting, and Staging Tradition for a Sustainable Future in Cultural Tourism in the Tsumkwe District of Namibia.* Zürich: Lit Verlag.

7 Goffman, Erving (1959): *Presentation of self in everyday life.* New York: Doubleday Anchor Books.

8 Ibid.

9 Nyani, Henry/ui, *Interview*, 11 January 2014 in Grashoek, Namibia, by Zips-Mairitsch, Manuela/Zips, Werner. Khau, Morris//oce, *Interview*, 17 January 2014 in Grashoek, Namibia, by Palekaite, Goda.

10 Parcher, Bruce, *Interview*, 13 January 2014 in Tsumkwe, Namibia, by Vestere, Elina/Koch, Julia/Kofi, Naa-Ansah/Kainz, Petra.

11 Cf. Zips-Mairitsch (2009): *Lost Lands?*, p. 22.

12 !L/ae, Tsemkgao – Smallboy, *Interview*, 15 January 2014 in Tsumkwe, Namibia, by Spitaler, Anna/Arienti, Valentina.

13 The term "Bushmen" used generically for the San people dates back to Dutch settlers in the 17th century, related to their natural environment and was used without questioning until the 1930's. A series of connotations attached to the term relating to "uncivilised" and "primitive", yet "Bushmen" is often heard up to the present. In the 1960's "The Harvard Kalahari Research Group" proposed to replace the ethically and gender discriminating term with "San", a relatively neutral Nama word that relies on their gathering-activity. See Zips-Mairitsch (2009): *Lost Lands?*, p. 156.

14 Silvester, Jeremy, *Interview*, 12 August 2014 in Windhoek, Namibia, by Wukovits, Josef/Ritterband, Salomé.

15 Cf. Garland, Elizabeth/Gordon, Robert J. (1999): *The Authentic (In)Authentic: Bushman. Anthro-Tourism.* In: Visual Anthropology, Vol. 12 (2), pp. 267–287, p. 268.

16 Ibid., p. 271.

17 Cf. ibid., p. 272.

18 Ibid., p. 268.

19 Cf. Stronza, Amanda (2001): *Anthropology of Tourism: Forging New Ground for Ecotourism and Other Alternatives.* In: Annual Review of Anthropology, Vol. 30, pp. 261–283, pp. 268–269.

20 Cf. ibid., p. 268–270.

21 Ibid., p. 271.

22 Cf. ibid., pp. 272–273.

23 Cf. ibid., p. 267.

24 Cf. ibid., p. 273.

25 Cf. Biesele/Hitchcock (2011): *The Ju/'hoan San of Nyae Nyae*, p. 101.

26 Cf. Hitchcock, Robert K. (1997): *Cultural, Economic and Environmental Impacts of Tourism Among Kalahari Bushmen.* In: Chambers, Erve (ed.): Tourism and Culture: An Applied Perspective. Albany: State University of New York Press, pp. 93–128, p. 94.

27 Cf. ibid., pp. 100–107.

28 Cf. Goodwin, Harold (2007): *Indigenous Tourism and Poverty Reduction.* In: Butler, Richard/Hinch, Thomas (ed.): Tourism and Indigenous Peoples: Issues and Implications. Oxford: Butterworth-Heinemann, pp. 84–94, pp. 84–85.

29 Cf. ibid., pp. 88–89.

30 Cf. Tomaselli, Keyan G. (2012): *Making Sense of the Indigenous: Who's Looking at Whom?* In: Tomaselli, Keyan G. (ed.): Cultural Tourism and Identity. Rethinking Indigeneity. Leiden: Koninklijke Brill NV, pp. 17–28, p. 18.

31 Stronza (2001): *Anthropology of Tourism*, p. 274.

32 Cf. McLennan-Dodd, Vanessa/Barnabas, Shanade (2012): *Shifting Representations of the Bushmen.* In: Tomaselli, Keyan G. (ed.): Cultural Tourism and Identity. Rethinking Indigeneity. Leiden: Koninklijke Brill NV. pp. 71–84, p. 39, 42–43.

33 Zips-Mairitsch (2009): *Lost Lands?* p. 254, 261.

34 Cf. Biesele/Hitchcock (2011): *The Ju/'hoan San of Nyae Nyae*, p. 100.

35 Cf. Garland/Gordon (1999): *The Authentic (In)Authentic*, p. 267.

36 Cf. Namibia Tourism Board (2013): *Namibia Tourism Satellite Account Report 2012*, 4th edition, p. 20. Available from: http://www.namibiatourism.com.na/uploads/file_uploads/TSA_2012_Report.pdf.

37 Cf. Biesele/Hitchcock (2011): *The Ju/'hoan San of Nyae Nyae*, p. 100.

38   Cf. Zips-Mairitsch (2009): *Lost Lands?* p. 154.

39   Cf. Suzman (2001): *Status of the San,* p. 80.

40   Cf. ibid., p. 85.

41   Ibid., p. 87.

42   Cf. Biesele/Hitchcock (2011): *The Ju/'hoan San of Nyae Nyae,* pp. 201–203.

43   Cf. ibid., pp. 209–210.

44   Cf. Suzman (2001): *Status of the San,* p. 41.

45   Cf. ibid., p. 39.

46   Cf. ibid., p. 138.

47   Cf. ibid., p. 134.

48   Cgaesje, Xoan//a and Cgaesje, !uu, *Interview*, 13 January 2014 in Doupos, Namibia, by Ritterband, Salomé.

49   Pfeifer, Werner, *Interview*, 9 January 2014 in Windhoek, Namibia, by Zips-Mairitsch, Manuela/ Zips, Werner.

50   Dürrschmidt, Sebastian, *Interview*, 13 August 2014 in Windhoek, Namibia, by Wukovits, Josef/ Ritterband, Salomé.

51   Daqm, Komtsa, *Interview*, 17 January 2014 in //Xa/oba, Namibia, by Kemelklyte, Dora/Pucher, Julia/Arienti, Valentina.

52   Von Stauss, Alexandra (2012): *Intercultural Encounters: the Kalahari and the Zulus.* In: Tomaselli, Keyan G. (ed.): Cultural Tourism and Identity. Rethinking Indigeneity. Leiden: Koninklijke Brill NV, pp. 85–98, p. 86.

53   MacCannell, Dean (1999 [1976]): *The Tourist.* New York: Schocken.

54   Urry, John (2002 [1990]): *The Tourist Gaze.* 2nd edition. London: Sage.

55   Von Stauss (2012): *Intercultural Encounters,* p. 86.

56   Ibid.

57   Cf. Goodwin (2007): *Indigenous Tourism,* p. 84.

58   Tomaselli, Keyan G. (2012): *What Have We Been Doing?* In: Tomaselli, Keyan G. (ed.): Cultural Tourism and Identity. Rethinking Indigeneity. Leiden: Koninklijke Brill NV. pp. 29–52, p. 31.

59   Cf. Disko, Stefan/Tugendhat, Helen (2014): *World Heritage Sites and Indigenous Peoples' Rights.* Copenhagen: IWGIA – Document 129, p. 11.

60   Cf. Butler, Richard/Hinch, Thomas (2007): *Introduction.* In: Butler, Richard/Hinch; Thomas (eds.): Tourism and Indigenous Peoples: Issues and Implications. Oxford: Butterworth-Heinemann. pp. 1–12, pp. 5–6.

61   Living Culture Foundation Namibia. Available from: http://www.lcfn.info/ [10.01.2016].

62   Dürrschmidt, Sebastian, *Interview*, 13 August 2014.

63   Cf. Comaroff/Comaroff (2009): *Ethnicity, Inc,* pp. 17–19.

64   Cf. Waitt, Gordon (1999): *Naturalizing the 'Primitive': A Critique of Marketing Australia's Indigenous Peoples as 'Hunter-Gatherers'.* In: Tourism Geographies: An International Journal of Tourism Space, Place and Environment, Vol. 1 (2), pp. 142–163, p. 147.

65   Akuupa, Michael Uusiku, *Interview*, 13 August 2014 in Katutura, Namibia, by Wukovits, Josef/ Ritterband, Salomé.

66   Cf. Layton, Robert/Wallace, Gillian (2006): *Is Culture a Commodity?* In: Layton, Robert/Wallace, Gillian (eds.): The Ethics of Archaeology. Philosophical Perspectives on Archaeological Practice. UK: Cambridge University Press, pp. 46–68.

67   Cf. Comaroff/Comaroff (2009): *Ethnicity, Inc,* p. 22.

68   Cf. ibid., p. 33.

69   N!aice, !amace, *Interview*, 16 January 2014 in //Xa/oba, Namibia, by Ritterband, Salomé/Erhart, Eva. Daqm, Tsemkgao, *Interview*, 17 January 2014 in //Xa/oba, Namibia, by Vestere, Elina. Komtsa, N!ae, *Interview*, 17 January 2014 in //Xa/oba, Namibia, by Tomancok, Anna-Sophie. /ui, Kxore Erna, *Interview*, 13 January 2014 in Grashoek, Namibia, by Katchikian, Alicja/Strasser, Silja.

70   Nyani, Henry /ui and N/aice, /Gao, *Interview*, 11 January 2014 in Grashoek, Namibia, by Tomancok, Anna-Sophie/Strasser, Silja.

71   Nyani, Henry/ui, *Interview*, 11 January 2014.

72   Cf. Silvester, Jeremy (2011): *Trading in Tradition: The Development of Cultural Villages in Namibia.* Unpublished Paper presented at the Commonwealth Association of Museums (CAM) Triennial

Conference "Commonwealth Museums: Culture, Economy and Climate Change and Youth", pp. 25–28. Available from: http://www.maltwood.uvic.ca/cam/publications/conference_publications/Jeremy%20Silvester.pdf.

73 Cf. ibid.

74 Silvester, Jeremy, *Interview*, 12 August 2014 in Windhoek, Namibia, by Wukovits, Josef/Ritterband, Salomé.

75 Dürrschmidt, Sebastian, *Interview*, 13 August 2014.

76 Dürrschmidt, Sebastian, *Private Lecture and Introduction* [unpublished], 9 January 2014 at LCFN, Windhoek.

77 Living Culture Foundation Namibia. Available from: http://www.lcfn.info/.

78 Khau, Morris //oce, *Interview*, 17 January 2014.

79 Ibid.

80 Cf. Taylor, Diana (2003): *The Archive and the Repertoire. Performing Cultural Memory in the Americas.* Durham/London: Duke University Press.

81 Daqm, Tsemkgao, *Interview*, 16 January 2014 in //Xa/oba, Namibia, by Erhart, Eva/Ritterband, Salomé.

82 Cf. Schechner, Richard (2013 [2002]): *Performance Studies: An Introduction.* 3rd edition. New York: Routledge.

83 Cf. ibid., pp. 228–229.

84 Cf. Bourdieu, Pierre (1982): *Die feinen Unterschiede. Kritik der gesellschaftlichen Urteilskraft.* Suhrkamp: Frankfurt am Main.

85 Schechner (2013): *Performance Studies*, p. 38.

86 Cf. Lewis, Lowell J. (2013): *The Anthropology of Cultural Performance.* New York: Palgrave Macmillan.

87 Bourdieu, Pierre (1977): *Outline of a Theory of a Practice.* Cambridge: Cambridge University Press.

88 Cf. Schechner (2013): *Performance Studies*, p. 93.

89 Cf. ibid., p. 228.

90 Cf. Lancy, David F./Bock, John/Gaskins, Suzanne (2010): *Putting Learning in Context.* In: Lancy, David F./Bock, John/Gaskins, Suzanne (eds.): The Anthropology of Learning in Childhood. UK: Alta Mira Press, pp. 3–5.

91 Cf. Gaskins, Suzanne/Paradise, Ruth (2010): *Learning through Observation in Daily Life.* In: Lancy et.al. (eds.): The Anthropology of Learning in Childhood. UK: Alta Mira Press, pp. 85–86.

92 Cf. Bourdieu (1977): *Outline of a Theory of a Practice*, p. 87.

93 Cf. ibid., p. 91, 106.

94 Cf. Lewis (2013): *The Anthropology of Cultural Performance*, p. 92.

95 Bourdieu (1977): *Outline of a Theory of a Practice.*

96 Komtsa, N!ae, *Interview*, 17 January 2014.

97 Cf. Katz, Richard (1982): *Boiling Energy: Community Healing among the Kalahari !Kung.* Cambridge/London: Harvard University Press, p. 118.

98 Ibid.

99 Daqm, Tsemkgao, *Interview*, 16 January 2014.

100 Cf. Taylor, Diana (2003): *The Archive and the Repertoire,* p. 20.

101 Cf. Schechner (2013): *Performance Studies.*

102 Cf. Lewis (2013): *The Anthropology of Cultural Performance*, p. 20.

103 Cf. Bourdieu (1977): *Outline of a Theory of a Practice*, pp. 87–88.

104 Daqm, Tsemkgao, *Interview*, 16 January 2014.

105 "Good morning!" in Ju/'hoansi

106 *Tjona* is the traditional leather trouser of the Ju/'hoansi worn by men.

107 The duiker is a medium-sized antelope that is used for meat and clothing production by the Ju/'hoansi San.

108 Ritterband, Salomé (2014): *Field Notes* [unpublished]. Doupos, Tsumkwe, Windhoek, 5. August – 10. September 2014.

109 For more information: http://www.namibiaforeningen.no/san-education-project.4612912-138547.html [13.05.2016].

110 Parcher, Bruce, *Interview*, 13 January 2014.

111 Cf. Lancy/Bock/Gaskins (2010): *Putting Learning in Context*, pp. 3–5.

112 Cf. Schechner (2013): *Performance Studies*, p. 228.

113 Cf. Lewis (2013): *The Anthropology of Cultural Performance*, p. 19.

114 Cf. Gray, Peter (2009): *Play as a Foundation for Hunter Gatherer Social Existence*. In: American Journal of Play, Vol. 1 (4), pp. 476–522, p. 505.

115 Cf. ibid., p. 510.

116 Cf. ibid., pp. 505–506.

117 Cf. Katz, Richard/Biesele, Megan/St. Denis, Verena (1997, eds.): *Healing Makes our Hearts Happy: Spirtuality and Cultural Transformation among the Kalahari Ju/'hoansi*. Rochester: Inner Traditions, pp. 76–77.

118 Biesele/Hitchcock (2011): *The Ju/'hoan San of Nyae Nyae,* pp. 233–234.

119 Cf. Suzman (2001): *Status of the San,* p. 123.

120 Parcher, Bruce, *Interview*, 13 January 2014.

121 Simasiku, Memory, *Interview*, 16 January 2014 in Grashoek, Namibia, by Katchikian, Alicja.

122 Parcher, Bruce, *Interview*, 13 January 2014.

123 Simasiku, Memory, *Interview*, 16 January 2014.

124 Hausiku, Perpetwa, *Interview*, 16 January 2014 in Grashoek, Namibia, by Katchikian, Alicja.

125 Ibid.

126 Parcher, Bruce, *Interview*, 13 January 2014.

127 Ibid.

128 Simasiku, Memory, *Interview*, 16 January 2014.

129 Daqm, Tsemkgao, *Interview*, 16 January 2014.

130 Parcher, Bruce, *Interview*, 13 January 2014.

131 Cf. Taylor (2003): *The Archive and the Repertoire.*

132 Cf. Bourdieu (1982): *Die feinen Unterschiede.*

133 Cf. Comaroff/Comaroff (2009): *Ethnicity, Inc.*

134 Butler, Richard/Hinch, Thomas (2007): *Conclusion*. In: Butler, Richard/Hinch, Thomas (eds.): Tourism and Indigenous Peoples: Issues and Implications. Oxford: Butterworth-Heinemann, pp. 319–332, pp. 328–329.

135 !L/ae, Tsemkgao – Smallboy, *Interview*, 4 September 2014 in Tsumkwe, Namibia, by Wukovits, Josef/Ritterband, Salomé.

136 Butler, Richard/Hinch, Thomas (2007): *Conclusion*, p. 324.

Maria Katelieva

Social and cultural impacts of tourism: The Case of the Bulgarian Villages Gorno Draglishte and Dobarsko

Introduction

The purpose of this paper is to give an overview of the social and cultural impacts of tourism upon the local community, using the example of two Bulgarian villages, which are emerging destinations for rural tourism. This study was conducted as a Master's thesis in cultural and social anthropology and both the literature and the research methodology used are mainly from this discipline.

The main research goal is to capture the role of tourism in social and cultural changes, which occur in the local community. Which changes occur as result of the development of tourism and can we clearly identify whether they are positive or negative for the local community? Is it possible to talk about sustainable and responsible tourism, or does each encounter between hosts and guests leave negative traces in the local community? Since tourism is the fastest growing industry and very important for developing countries, it is important to analyse its impact and to manage it in a way that benefits the communities concerned. However, tourism should not be seen as a panacea for the problems of developing countries, its impact should not be overrated, but closely analysed, because sometimes there is no clear border between a negative and a positive impact. Since it is difficult to assess and quantify the social and cultural impact, the study uses qualitative methods, such as participant observation, participatory workshops, group interviews and in-depth interviews with tourism stakeholders, as well as some methods used in the social impact assessment (SIA), such as community profiles, stakeholder analysis, tourism development timeline, transect walks etc.

The fieldwork was carried out in the villages of Gorno Draglishte and Dobarsko in Bulgaria, which are in close proximity to the town of Bansko – an important destination for ski-tourism. In these villages, people have been hosting tourists for several years and they want tourism to grow and develop sustainably. These villages were selected because the size of the community is manageable, tourism is still developing and it is possible to not only capture existing impacts, but also to foresee and eventually prevent future negative impacts. Thus, this study is of relevance for the development of sustainable tourism in rural areas and has practical implications for stakeholders, who want to be aware of the social and cultural impact of tourism and want to maximize the benefit that can be gained from tourism.

Tourism research among anthropological studies

Tourism has been the research object of many anthropological studies and according to Stronza since tourism occurs in most human societies and this is one of the reasons why this topic "seems to occupy at least a subsection in many studies"[1]. Nash and Smith claim that the "official entry" for anthropologists into the field of tourism is the first edition of Hosts and Guests[2]. Anthropologists are interested in various issues related to tourism, such as the impact of tourism on the local culture or ethnicity, reasons and motivations for travel etc. In "Anthropology of Tourism" Burns proposes different key issues and main questions in tourism anthropology, such as "tourism as a new religion and pilgrimage", "tourism as a social change", "tourism as a myth – can tourism offer a paradise on earth?", "does tourism support the development of the local community?"[3]. Nash summarises the research questions in tourism anthropology in a similar way[4]. Nowadays there are many academic synergies between the research fields of social anthropology and tourism as both disciplines deal with culture and mobility. In order to define the impact of tourism on the local community, we first should look at the nature of tourism as a social phenomenon. In the literature on tourism, it was often said that tourists (especially in the case of ethnic tourism) left their home in order to search for "real life" elsewhere. MacCannell explains this very clearly:

> "The modernisation of work relations, history and nature detaches these from their traditional roots and transforms them into cultural productions and experiences [...]. Modern Man is losing his attachments to the work bench, the neighbourhood, the town, the family, which he once called 'his own', but at the same time, he is developing interest in the 'real life' of others."[5]

The desire to escape the everyday life, modern society and the mass produced goods is the reason to search for authentic experiences. According to Nash and Urry, modern society is characterised by superficial experiences and alienation, while traveling is a search for both diversity and something "real"[6]. This is also the paradox of modern mass tourism, which is one of the main sources of change in many traditional cultures and is the reason for the creation of so-called "pseudo-events" and "staged authenticity"[7]. Tourists are not only visitors of a country, but they are also consumers of its culture and can thus come in close contact with it when they are interested in cultural tourism, or their contact can remain superficial if they consume only the services of the tourist resort or all-inclusive packages. Burns argues that "tourism is a global set of activities, crossing many cultures"[8] and this is why the profound analysis of the consequences of the contacts between the visiting and the hosting communities is very important. According to Stronza there has been a shift in anthropological literature on tourism, and while anthropologists used to be more critical towards tourism in the past, now "the tendency seems to be to applaud tourism as a panacea for achieving a wide array of social, economic, and environmental goals"[9].

Sustainable/responsible tourism

The United Nations Environment Programme (UNEP) and the World Tourism Organisation (WTO) define sustainable tourism as "tourism that takes full account of its current and future economic, social and environmental impacts, addressing the needs of visitors, the industry, the environment and host communities"[10]. According to the UNEP and WTO, all forms of tourism in different destinations could become more sustainable if the management is focused on striking a balance between the three most important aspects of sustainability: the environmental, economic, and socio-cultural aspects. Moreover, sustainable tourism should:

> *"1) Make optimal use of environmental resources that constitute a key element in tourism development, maintaining essential ecological processes and helping to conserve natural heritage and biodiversity; 2) Respect the socio-cultural authenticity of host communities, conserve their built and living cultural heritage and traditional values, and contribute to inter-cultural understanding and tolerance; 3) Ensure viable, long-term economic operations, providing socio-economic benefits to all stakeholders that are fairly distributed, including stable employment and income-earning opportunities and social services to host communities, and contributing to poverty alleviation"[11].*

Tourism contributes to the economic development and quality of life of locals, but very often expectations are too high and tourism is seen as a panacea for development problems. Goodwin claims that tourism can make a significant contribution to the UN Millennium Development Goals and for the reduction of poverty. However, the challenge is to create indicators and systems to measure its impact.[12]

The different ways in which tourism affects the host community and its culture are even more difficult to capture and cannot be measured, but they also depend on the level of sustainability of the tourism development. Social and cultural changes can be caused directly by contact with incoming tourists, but may also be due to the local tourism industry, which seeks to adapt conditions to tourists' needs. The tourism industry can manage social and cultural changes in a sustainable way by monitoring the number of tourists and sustainably managing the offering available for tourists (e.g. by including and empowering the local community). In the best-case scenario, tourism is community-based and locals provide services and products in their own enterprises, using at least one part of their income for projects, which provide benefits to the community as a whole.

Most studies on the social and cultural impact of tourism have been conducted in developing countries, which have become leading tourist destinations in recent decades. Since tourism causes encounters between different cultures and levels of living standards, it is often considered to be the main cause of changes in the way of life of local communities. In more developed countries and modern societies, it is particularly difficult to distinguish between changes caused by tourism and those caused by the overall process of globalisation. However, potential negative and positive impacts must be taken into account when managing tourism in a given destination. In many cases, it is difficult to determine whether an impact is negative or positive, as there could be a conflict between socio-economic development and the conservation of culture or nature. Opposing interests may also arise within the local community, or between the community and external organisations and companies involved in tourism. In any case, it is crucial for the sustainable development of tourism to clarify and consider priorities for the local community and maintain the balance between the community, its economy, culture and nature.

Different types of tourists and the host – guest relations

According to Smith and Burns, the impact on local culture depends not only on the number of tourists, but also on the reason behind their journey and their ability to adapt.[13] Smith offers the following typology of tourists (Table 1), in which the number is inversely proportional to the adaptation to local conditions. "Explorer", according to the author, are rather close to anthropologists who merge with the locals and participate actively in their daily lives, and gradual growth towards mass tourism leads to the introduction of "western" amenities and changes in lifestyle.

Type of tourist	Numbers of tourists	Adaptation to local norms
Explorer	Very limited	Accepts fully
Elite	Rarely seen	Adapts fully
Off-beat	Uncommon but seen	Adapts well
Unusual	Occasional	Adapts somewhat
Incipient mass	Steady flow	Seeks western amenities
Mass	Continuous influx	Expects western amenities
Charter	Mass arrivals	Demands western amenities

Table 1. Frequency of types of tourists and their adaptations to local norms.[14]

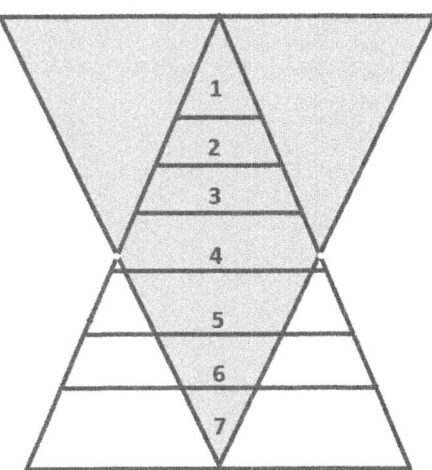

Image 1. Touristic impact upon culture (white triangle) and local perceptions of visitors (grey triangle) expressed by types of tourism[15]: 1. Explorer, 2. Elite, 3. Off-beat, 4. Unusual, 5. Incipient mass, 6. Mass, 7. Charter

In other studies tourists are categorised in different types according to the reason behind them wanting to experience a different culture and the level and depth of cultural experience sought.

The term "encounter" has been used by most researchers, when they talk about the contact between tourists and locals, because they want to emphasise the personal interaction. Krippendorf highlights that in sustainable tourism this encounter should be characterised by a mutual interest and desire for understanding and acceptance through mutual respect and attention[16]. Different social statuses and roles in this encounter should also be considered: the tourist is mobile, relaxed, enjoys his spare time and his experience of the different place. However, the hosts are relatively stationary and, if employed in the tourism industry, spend much of their time serving the needs and desires of visitors. The type of the encounter and interaction between hosts and guests also depends on the characteristics of the social groups they belong to, as well as on the situation in which the contact is taking place.

Mathieson and Wall suggest three main types of situations when hosts and guests might come into direct contact: when the tourist buys a good or service from the host; when the guest and host are next to each other (e.g. on the beach); when they communicate in order to exchange information and ideas.[17] The mutual respect and interest in the other culture is one of the main features of sustainable tourism and a characteristic of the tourists, who travel responsibly.

There are a number of impacts on the locals' lifestyle, value systems and traditions that are caused by the encounter between locals in developing countries and the western society, and since many researchers define tourism as "the fastest growing industry", tourists are often seen as the main agents of cultural change.

However, it is important to take into account other mass forms of intercultural communication in the modern world, such as media or migration, and try to distinguish them from the role of tourism. Burns argues that cultural change can be triggered either by the internal evolution of a society, driven by the needs of capitalism, or forced by external economic, ecological and cultural influences[18]. Development is a major characteristic of culture and there are no cultures, which have remained unaltered. Wood also sees tourism as one of many social that impacts upon culture in different ways and believes that tourism itself does not have the power to destroy culture, nor to preserve it[19].

Case Study Sites Gorno Draglishte and Dobarsko

Fieldwork Methodology

Fieldwork of four weeks in total was conducted for this study. Participatory workshops, key informant interviews and transect walks were the main methods used for the qualitative research approach. In order to capture the impact on the community, based on the stakeholder theory, it was important to identify all the key stakeholders and interest groups. According to Byrd

> "stakeholder theory can describe the multiple elements of tourism in a community, the history of tourism development in the community, the procedures and policies that relate to the development and management of tourism in the area, the types of attractions in the community, the overall economic impact to the community, the size of the tourism industry in the community, and the connections between the different agencies and organisations that are involved in tourism"[20].

In order to capture and understand these elements, different stakeholders were contacted, such as owners of guesthouses, mayors of the villages, managers of tour operators, tourist guides, random people from the community and tourists etc. Participatory workshops with the owners of several guesthouses, as well as other people involved in tourism, were organised in order to identify the important tourism stakeholders, their relationships and their interests and opinions on sustainable tourism issues. Individual interviews were conducted with some of the guesthouses' owners, the mayors of Gorno Draglishte and Dobarsko, representatives of the two tourist companies, which organise guided tours to the villages, tour guides and the "Babi" (Grandmothers) of Gorno Draglishte, who are responsible for the folklore programme that is offered to tourists. In the empirical material, I also include paraphrased statements or short quotations from conversations, which have been recorded in my field diary (with people in the Gorno Draglishte pub, women participating in the folklore program, tourists and the owners of some guesthouses). Transect walks together with some of the key informants helped to map the community and define the most common places and sights where tourists meet the locals. In my field diary I also kept notes from the participant observations of the encounter between the hosts and the guests, the folklore program, which is offered to the guests, the demonstrations of some traditions, some guided hiking tours and visits to local sights, the village fair in Gorno Draglishte and others.

Gorno Draglishte – community profile

The village is located in the northern part of the Razlog valley, 13 km from the town of Razlog and 10 km from the ski resort Bansko. The village is electrified, has a water-supply and the streets are partially asphalted.

Population: 900 people (290 houses)
Religion: mostly Orthodox Christians
Ethnicity: Bulgarians (there are two Roma families)
Main source of income: agriculture, livestock, timber, tourism (people also work in hotels in Bansko)
Migration: Some families work seasonally abroad, 5 families have moved permanently, many young people work in Razlog (a bigger town) and Bansko; there are three families who do not live here permanently and use their houses as holiday homes
Tourist resources: guest houses, restaurants, cafes and shops, "Valiavitsa" as a cultural landmark, walking hiking trails and a waterfall (25 m) in Rila National Park, folklore group performances, 100-year-old tree, a cave
Number of tourists per year: No information; most of them, over 70% of all the overnight stays are made by tourists from two tourist companies from Sofia
Major tourist seasons: June – August (summer) and December – April (winter)
Transportation: 7 daily buses from Razlog (including the school bus)
Educational and health facilities: The village has a kindergarten, elementary school (high school in Razlog), dentist, doctor and a cultural centre (male and female folk group and a football club).

There is no local organisation for regulation, management and decision-making regarding tourism. The development of tourism is largely due to tourist companies from Sofia and projects to Razlog and Bansko.

Timeline of tourism development in Gorno Draglishte – main events:
1989 the communist regime fell.
1990 consultants funded by the Swiss project and USAID provide training for the development of guest houses and tourism.
2003 the Swiss project ends.
2004 the first guest arrived at Guesthouse Deshka (not a certified guesthouse yet).

2005 the first certified guesthouses were set up in Gorno Draglishte (guesthouse Deshka).

2007 The first organised tourist groups arrive (initially two tourist companies sent groups but now there are more companies).

2009 Bansko tour operators start to host guests from Bansko hotels on day trips to Gorno Draglishte in order to show them the rural lifestyle.

Dobarsko – community profile

The village is situated at an altitude of 1050 m above sea level, 18 km from the town of Razlog and 17 km from the town of Bansko.

Population: 650 people
Religion: mostly Orthodox Christians
Ethnicity: Bulgarians
Main source of income: agriculture, livestock, timber, tourism
Migration: seasonal workers in Greece
Tourist resources: Medieval church "St. Teodor Tiron and Teodor Stratilat" (part of the 100 national tourist sites of Bulgaria – a list of the most important cultural sights), walking hiking trails, folk performances by "Dobarski Babi" (folklore group), presentation of a traditional Bulgarian wedding ceremony and "feruglitsa" (sewing of a traditional wedding flag), celebration of St. Varvara with a festive fire (December)
Major tourist seasons: June – August (summer) and December – April (winter)

Timeline of tourism development in Dobarsko:
1977 Church in Dobarsko is declared a cultural monument – visitors come but do not stay in the village
2003 Nina Baikova creates an initiative group for the development of tourism in Dobarsko
2005 project funding is received
2005 BAAT introduces the category of guest house in the categorisation of accommodation and the first houses start to work legally (Originally there were more houses but now there are four: Vassil House, Makedonka House, Radi House, Villa House)
2008 the church is listed as a place of interest by the National History Museum

Results: Cultural and social impact of tourism

Among tourism researchers and cultural anthropologists it is often discussed whether tourism can lead to cultural changes and especially negative ones, such as destroying local traditions, adopting negative patterns of behaviour, conflicts between different groups in the community or changes in values (for example, shifting focus from the family, religion and the community to the "hedonistic" lifestyle of tourists). Critics see tourism as an acculturation process in which the cultures of developing countries adapt to the "materialistic" lifestyle of the western world. *Acculturation* is a process in which one or more elements of one culture (usually more economically developed) are "borrowed" by the other culture as result of their contact, which may be of a different duration.[21]

Thus, according to Nash, the host community adapts, seeks to satisfy the tourists' needs and respects the attitudes and values of the guests meaning that the hosts' culture begins to look more like the tourists' culture[22]. Burns believes that this exchange process is not balanced (the hosts do not always aspire assume the culture of the guests) and the stronger culture dominates and begins to change the weaker (not to say lower) culture by reflecting itself onto it in a mirror-like process[23]. The process of acculturation can be observed through hybridisation or the "demonstration effect"[24]. Hybridisation refers to the process where two cultures are brought together and a culture is formed (also known as creolisation). The effect of the demonstration was described by Burns as "the process by which traditional societies, especially those who are particularly susceptible to outside influences such as youth, will voluntarily willingly seek to adopt certain behaviours" with the expectation that this will provide them "the leisured, hedonistic lifestyle demonstrated by the tourists"[25]. While the so called "demonstration effect" is typical for traditional societies and cannot be observed in the case of Gorno Draglishte and Dobarsko, there are some other indications of acculturation and hybridity of the local lifestyle. Some of the local hosts for instance do not approve of the depiction of a rural lifestyle seen in the guesthouses or through their local dialect and way of life, and try to create a modern setting in their houses, aspiring to the living standard of their guests. Different statements like "we need/want to change" are sometimes mentioned by locals during the discussions about attracting tourists. The "change" mentioned here is in terms of adapting houses and lifestyle to the needs of the tourists, as well as learning how to provide services and studying foreign languages.

One of the most feared negative impacts of tourism is the *commoditisation of local culture*. The term, which means transformation into a commodity, is a process whereby a subject or element of the culture is valued according to the level of interest it raises[26]. This process can lead to a decrease of its importance to the local community (for example, performing a certain ritual doesn't have the same meaning anymore). MacCannell argues that material and spiritual traditions interact with tourists at the commercial level, culture undergoes a process of turning into commodity under the influence of tourists who are making a "production" or a "fetish" of the rural village life or the "traditional domestic relations"[27]. MacCannell compares the "all-consuming tourist" symbolically with a cannibal as tourists consume not only resources and material goods, but the cultures they meet[28]. Another example is provided by Mowforth and Munt, who reveal the general trend that Maasai, Maya, and other indigenous groups are seen as objects in a "human museum showcase" and they call this "zooification" of the tribal peoples[29]. In the case of Gorno Draglishte and Dobarsko, the local folklore is being turned into kind of a product. Wood also argues that international tourism "reinforces the objectification of culture"[30].

The local dialect in particular is very interesting for people who understand Bulgarian and the locals are aware of that. In the house of the key informant Deshka there is a folklore programme for the guests, which consists of traditional folklore songs, dance workshops, cooking and weaving lessons amongst other handicrafts. The main actors in this programme are the host's mother and her friends, who are the so-called "Babi" (grandmothers) of Gorno Draglishte. It is important to discuss where border lies between selling what you do (lessons, handicrafts, songs, dances) and selling what you are (hospitality, dialect).

On the other hand, Krippendorf illustrates how tourists are also treated as objects and while meeting the new culture is an exciting experience to them, to the locals it is just another repetition of the same situation. When describing mass tourism, Krippendorf argues that it cannot represent a meaningful and worthy encounter between guests and hosts and that the contact is superficial, if for the host community profit is the primary goal or if there is the feeling of inferiority and superiority in the communication. Krippendorf then uses this as a basis for creating the concepts of "humane" "mild" (sanft) or "responsible" tourism that take into account environmental protection and the needs and rights of all those involved in tourism.[31]

One of the characteristics of sustainable and responsible tourism is the positive experience of the encounter for both sides. *The escape from everyday* sought by the tourists can be also relevant for locals as cultural dialogue is a mutual process. If for tourists, the visit to a new place is an "escape" from their usual habitat and everyday life, for some hosts meeting different people and cultures is a kind of "journey" without physical relocation. Despite the relatively routine process of tourism service, these meetings can be unique and varied, however this depends on the number and type of tourists visiting the community as well as the willingness of locals to have close and free contact. The communication with the tourists is perceived in a very positive manner by the "Babi" in Gorno Draglishte. They say that the guests diversify their everyday life and distract them from their daily problems:

> "This is our way to have fun, there is no time to think about problems, loans …
> and there are enough problems", "when they say 'let's go to Deshka' I am always
> ready, I do not want to leave"; "I'm a little bit sad when they (the guesthouse
> owners) don't call me to come. When there is no tourist group for a longer
> time"; "the village is alive, there is always singing and dancing in the street".[32]

The issue of *changes to local identity* is also linked to "selling" and presenting local culture. Is local identity vanishing due to tourism or is it being created by developing an image as a destination? Many tourist organisations oversee the sustainable development of tourism share the opinion that the attempts of the local population to adapt the atmosphere and the conditions to the demands of tourists lead to homogenisation and a loss of cultural identity.

As already mentioned in Gorno Draglishte owners of different guesthouses have different opinions on how the village should be presented to and perceived by visitors. Over the years, Deshka's house has become popular with its casual home atmosphere, delicious homemade cuisine and local dialect, other guesthouses have adopted a similar way of presenting themselves. Some other hosts try to offer luxury accommodation and do not want to be seen as and are even offended by the term "farmers" or "villagers".

An interesting case in point is the hotel Pirila in Gorno Draglishte, whose owners are from England and have lived in the village since 2006. The hosts prepare traditional Bulgarian dishes themselves, but unlike other guesthouses, they do not offer a folklore programme: *"we show them just the rural life, without going into details about culture because we do not know it enough. But to our guests it is enough to meet the Bulgarian village, which is so different and relaxed"*[33]. They present Bulgarian rural life without emphasising the traditions, folklore and history. As they themselves were initially tourists and remain very impressed by the peaceful rural life, they consider this interesting and attractive enough for foreign tourists: *"British people love the Bulgarian village because it is like our villages 60 years ago. They admire the fact that people grow their own vegetables because in England almost no one is doing it anymore"*[34]. From other conversations with tourists it also becomes clear that they are very impressed by the fact that "people cut the grass with a scythe", "they travel by horse and carts", or "cook on wood stoves". These are things, which remind them of their childhood and trigger a pleasant sense of nostalgia for the past in their countries. In the brochures of one of the companies offering the trips to Gorno Draglishte and Dobarsko they present the villages as "villages, which preserved the rhythm of life from a few centuries ago" but one of their tour guides also says:

> *"We cannot wish or expect from the locals to live like centuries ago, stay 'authentic' without any development, so that tourists can go there and feel well. And the traditions, they should be there if they are needed and if people believe in them."*[35]

If we assume that cultural identity is the result of past historical events, but also the fruit of modern times, we will agree that it cannot remain constant. The problem of homogenisation exists mainly in large mass tourism resorts, where the services are standardised and there are almost no specific features of the respective culture. In small settlements (excluding artificially created tourist villages), where tourism develops sustainably, local identity is preserved in order to attract visitors and some traditions are even being artificially constructed or "invented".[36] Therefore, if homogenisation occurs as part of the process of globalisation, it is sometimes tourist industry that creates the "new" local identity. Many of the popular tourist destinations today owe their identity to travellers from the past. In his book "The Art of Travel", British journalist Alan de Botton explains the symbolic meaning of places visited by famous writers and artists (e.g. Gustave Flaubert, Van Gogh, Edward Hopper, Alexander von Humboldt, John Ruskin, etc.), who make these places popular by mythologising them in their art or literature. De Botton argues for instance that the popularity of the Provence region is largely due to Van Gogh's paintings. The so-called mediators between the local community and the guests play an important role in shaping local identity – they can be tourist companies as well as journalists and authors of tourist literature.[37]

Furthermore, it is relevant to ask whether tourism leads to *destroying or preserving traditions*. The development of tourism and the local community while preserving culture and traditions is one of the key objectives of the Cape Town Declaration[38], but in many cases the balance of the two objectives is difficult. It is legitimate to ask why traditions are being artificially maintained, if the locals do not need certain practices or customs anymore. Will they continue to have the same function as they used to, or will they serve only to attract tourists? The coexistence of economic development and modernisation, and the preservation of culture and traditions, is maybe possible if we look at McKean's theory of *"cultural involution"*[39]. He borrows the term "involution" from Geertz's "Agrarian Involution"[40]. McKean adapts the term to culture, noting that the community can evolve and undergo socio-cultural development by returning to tradition. Traditional crafts, songs and dances attract tourists and the development of tourism leads to the development and innovation needed by society to adapt to modern reality. Thus, traditional practices, rituals etc. play a new important role for the local community by supporting its economic development. In terms of material culture, commoditisation is often seen in the production of souvenirs. Shepherd mentions the discussion among tourism critics on the "reductions in the aesthetic quality of cultural products and traditions due to tourist demands"[41], which is visible in the products of the material culture. Kasfir explains for instance that the change in the Samburu warrior's spear – the "miniaturisation of the tourist spear"[42] which is traditionally taller than the warrior, is made in order to be transportable by tourists. In this case study the author emphasises the change of the function of the object after being visually changed and brought to another place for the act of sale: "this removal of the spear from its usual place and from its socially embedded position, and the alterations to its scale and decoration are all necessary in order to defuse its power and reinvent it as a neutral object for a new clientele and a different purpose."[43] Thus, the spear is no longer a weapon or a material culture, but an aesthetic object, a souvenir.

The function of these *reinvented traditions* is now to attract and entertain tourists, and thus to provide income for the locals. It can be argued that it is a commoditisation of culture but in some cases the reinvented culture elements have been forgotten or even denied by locals before being reinvented for tourism purposes. A good example from Gorno Draglishte is the "hamkane" (catching food with mouth) custom of the "Zagovezny" celebration: the oldest person in the family ties an egg with a string and spins it while the children try to catch it using only their mouths. When showing this custom to the tourists, the hosts argue that the string should be a red one and one of them said *"Maybe it is, I never did it."* Another example is the sewing of the wedding "ferruglitsa" (wedding flag) in Dobarsko where the "tradition" is no longer related to weddings, but is presented when there is a group of tourists who want to see it. Although deprived of their former significance and symbolism, these traditions now do not only serve a commercial function. The invention of traditions turns into the daily work of women in the folk ensemble because they always think of new reinventions and versions of traditions they can use in order to keep the tourists entertained:

> *"I want to come up with something new"; "For the adults it is difficult, I keep thinking all night long"; "we often gather and sing, every week when a group comes, otherwise we rehearse, we think, here we have our new songs".*[44]

It is also interesting to note the change in the attitudes of locals towards traditional handicrafts. According to one of the hosts, most people in the village were not interested in traditional handicrafts until it became clear that they could be a source of income:

> *"When I started to make my crafts workshop everybody was saying I was out of my mind, because I was collecting all the junk – 'razboj', 'vrutka' (different traditional tools), things like these… so for them it was not interesting."*[45]

A positive impact on the local community may be the *higher appreciation that locals gain for themselves and their culture* as result of the contact with guests. Boissevain argues that the tourists' interest in the local culture triggers the pride and the self-confidence of the hosts[46]. Burns suggests that the contact between hosts and guests increases the self-confidence of the hosts[47]. The appreciation which comes from outside, leads to higher self-esteem within the host society. In the case of Gorno Draglishte the popularity of the village, attracts not only more tourists *"from all over the world"* but also the attention of Bulgarian national media. This attention leads to increased self-esteem and pride. In many cases, when asked *"What is the positive side of hosting tourists?"* locals answers are *"so many people come to you, although you are nobody", "the whole world comes to see us", "we do not need to go anywhere because the world comes to us", "we became famous".*[48] They often talk about the television crews, which come to film the "Babi" of Dobarsko (a local singing group) and a famous cooking show, which shot some cooking at Deshka's guesthouse for a week. The various places where tourists come from also give locals the feeling that they are interesting to the whole world. They often list the countries tourists come from:

> *"They come from Venezuela, from South Africa, from Japan"; "Germans, French, Romanians – they are almost like residents here"; "Well, there was that one man the other day … he was so dark, you could see only his white teeth".*[49]

The appreciation also becomes higher for the natural resources that local people often take for granted, which also leads to increased levels of care for nature and the environment. This can also happen with cultural heritage (tangible or intangible), which in many societies seeking modernisation has lost its importance and in some cases even become embarrassing (e.g. dialects or traditional clothing). As opposed to the claim that tourism is damaging culture, according to some researchers, tourism has the ability to maintain and revive local traditions. Smith as well as Phillips and Steiner point to a number of examples of craft industries in different indigenous communities, which show that tourism serves to revitalise traditional industries by providing a market for local products[50]. Boissevain also illustrates how turning culture into commodity enables some marginalised communities with declining populations to maintain their viability and local traditions[51].

Tourism development can also lead to a *higher levels of appreciation of natural resources and the environment*. According to the locals, the guests "teach" them many things related to environmental sustainability and nature conservation, such as waste management:

> *"They come and ask 'where to put that? Where do I dispose of this?' And I'm telling my husband 'Wow, it's a shame we put everything in one place' And you slowly change your mind. You throw something on the street, but you know there are people around you and you're thinking 'It's not right. I have to throw it into the bin'. "[52]*

The tourists' interest towards nature makes local people appreciate their natural wealth, take care of it and maintain the hiking trails and the surrounding area –

> *"And they also make us value what we are given – nature. Well, it's not only them, but it is important, when they say 'This is so beautiful!' and you know there are other countries who can only dream of what we have."[53]*

On the other hand, the development of tourism in the community and the reunification around such a common cause as the sustainable development and nature protection may reinforce the *community development and the social solidarity*. The concern of the local community for the natural and cultural heritage, as well as the striving to create an attractive destination image, can lead to strong social connections within the community.

The locals in Gorno Draglishte organise different *local initiatives*, such as cleaning and signposting the hiking trails, creating a nature conservation centre "for the protection of the wood grouse and the Rila primrose" in Dobarsko (with the help of the Razlog Municipality), the restoration and maintenance of the "valiavitsa" (a traditional facility for doing the laundry, which is an interesting sight) and the construction of a new chapel in Gorno Draglishte etc. Another important consequence of the local initiatives for revitalising local culture is also the increased levels of interest that children and young people show in terms their own culture. More and more children are starting to learn traditional dances in the local folklore group and some of the guesthouses organise handicraft or nature education workshops for the schools from the region. According to the participants in the stakeholder meeting, organised during the fieldwork, it is very important that *"children learn more about nature, about farmers' work, learn crafts and folk dances"*[54]. Some of the hosts are also very happy that their children have decided to stay in the village after graduating school and help with the family business. Many young people work in hotels in Bansko in the winter, but during the summer, they mostly work in their parents' guesthouses.

The issue of authenticity is central when we discuss the cultural impact of tourism. In search of the "authentic experience", tourists often do not realise that it is actually everywhere around them. If the purpose of the trip is to experience the foreign culture this happens all the time while tourists are among the locals (with their hosts, in the shops and restaurants, on the street). According to MacCannell, this lies in the contemporary perception of "real" and "true". What tourists expect to see, led by pictures in brochures, magazines, and movies, is precisely what MacCannell calls "staged authenticity", which local people create in order to satisfy the guests. MacCannell explains the concepts of authenticity and staged authenticity through the front- and backstage opposition which Goffmann uses to describe the structural division of social contacts and perceptions of "truth" and "reality" in modern society. This symbolic separation of space automatically surrounds the "backstage" in mystery and creates the feeling of something intimate, "authentic" and hidden from the guest's eye, distinguishing it from the "frontstage", which is a facade, stage and show for the tourists. In order to create a convincing "social reality" part of it must remain hidden. As an examples of the "backstage", MacCannell refers to the kitchens or laundry facilities in the tourist accommodation. However, it is sometimes difficult for the guest to distinguish the front- from the backstage, as the hosts skilfully construct the "staged authenticity" (e.g. when rooms in guesthouses are arranged with the hosts' personal belongings and create the feeling that these are their personal rooms).[55]

In their desire to create a "home setting", the hosts arrange the "scene" using personal items as well as others objects, which look like they were bought in souvenir shops. Here some pictures from one of the guesthouses are used in order to give a better idea of what a typical guesthouse in the village looks like. The tavern in the house is decorated in the typical style customary for Bulgarian taverns with traditional clothes and carpets on the walls and next to it is the "craft workshop" where guests learn to weave and knit. The atelier resembles a small ethnographic museum, yet it creates a homely feeling.

Image 2. Crafts workshop at Guesthouse Deshka © Maria Katelieva

Image 3. Letter from a guest at Guesthouse Deshka © Maria Katelieva

Image 4. The tavern/dining room at Guesthouse Deshka © Maria Katelieva

On the second floor, where the hosts' bedrooms are situated, there are family pictures on the walls and the traditional rural items are absent. The guest rooms are furnished just like the hosts bedrooms and on the shelves there are some of the belongings of the hosts. In another guesthouse in Dobarsko, the room is also decorated with traditional clothes and aprons woven by the host and the whole atmosphere of this dining room is more homely.

Image 5. Guesthouse in Dobarsko © Lucy McCombes

Image 6. The host Baba Rada (on the left) with her husband and a friend © Lucy McCombes

The way tourists are welcomed when they arrive and the folklore programme are also kind of "staged". In Gorno Draglishte and Dobarsko the "Babi" dressed in in traditional clothes welcome the guests with traditional bread, sing a song and give the tourists bouquets of geranium leaves (as a symbol of health). The folklore programme of some guesthouses consists of traditional songs, folk dances and tourists can dress up in traditional clothes.

Image 7. "Babi" in Draglishte and Dobarsko are preparing for the folklore programme © Guesthouse Deshka

Image 8. "Babi" in Draglishte and Dobarsko are preparing for the folklore programme
© *Guesthouse Deshka*

Image 9. "Babi" in Draglishte and Dobarsko are preparing for the folklore programme
© *Guesthouse Deshka*

Staged authenticity can be attributed not only to the shaping of space but also to all activities in the everyday life of the hosts, their clothing, rituals and more. According to Graburn tourists are the ones who are mainly concerned about "authenticity" and since authenticity is socially constructed "anthropologists have not considered authenticity to be an analytical category or a measure of culture, a people or their art forms"[56].

From the conversations with tourists in Gorno Draglishte it becomes clear that they perceive the experience in this village as very authentic. They can distinguish very well between the entertainment put on by the locals from the "show" for tourists, such as the folklore programmes in the guesthouses. This is why for instance they skip parts of their organised tours in order to participate in the traditional spring fair in Gorno Draglishte called "Sabor" (there is one in almost every village in Bulgaria – people gather and celebrate, friends and relatives from other villages come to visit). This is one of the few cases where tourists attend an event that is not specially prepared for them. For them this is a very special experience and for some locals (especially from the folk group, which is performing) it is an honour that guests choose the fair over visiting other sights. It can be said that this is one of the few cases in which guests enter "behind the scenes" of stage authenticity in which they are usually the audience. The more intimate nature of the village fair peaks the tourists' interest and provides for a unique experience.

However, in their search for the authentic experience, tourists often invade the private space in the everyday life of the hosts, which is described as the "backstage" away from the presence of tourists[57]. Boissevain discusses the different strategies host communities use to protect and even resist, hide or relocate their cultural festivals away from tourists, "locals only" rituals and events, organising protests and rejecting the development of tourism[58]. These examples raise the question of how far tourists should be allowed to enter the "privacy" of the community without invitation and whether tourism can be managed responsibly so that they guarantee the privacy and the rights of the local community.

This invasion of the private space is more present in the guesthouses, where hosts live together with their guests and are in contact with them every day:

> "There is no end of the workday, we are available 24 hours a day, otherwise it does not work. This job means you have not much time for yourself. You do not really have any private space, not even private rooms (laughs). Well, that's all right … this morning the whole tourist group wanted to come to the kitchen and see the cooking stove and I told them that it is not clean now, my sink is full of dishes! Not that I'm ashamed … so they came, took pictures of the stove (laughing). Haven't they seen a stove?"[59]

In some guesthouses, guests can go anywhere including in the kitchen. Some hosts also rent their own rooms and sleep somewhere else, if the groups are too big. So for instance, in the house of Baba Rada in Dobarsko the dining room is relocated to the kitchen where the guests eat together with the hosts and the whole house is open to the guests. Other hosts prefer to have separate rooms or floors for the hosts but they also spend their time with the guests.

The constant presence of tourists changes the life of the family, the hosts are constantly occupied and have less time for family occasions or holidays. They are mostly busy during the important holidays (Christmas, Easter) and spend their time taking care of the guests. Most owners of guesthouses do not travel and are permanently available because there are many tourists that arrive without a reservation and are looking for accommodation. However, the hosts' opinion is that this job is much more pleasant, enjoyable and diversified than other jobs they had in the past years:

> "It's fun, this job is fun. Years ago I used to work at the post office, then a cowherd, we had cows and beetroot and cucumbers, we did not have a break ... we cultivated mushrooms, we used to have a bakery for ten years. I was also a seamstress. I still pay the rent for my workshop because I do not know what will happen in the future and there is so much equipment. But the guesthouse is the most important thing now. This is the most pleasant thing, tourism…and there is no explanation, I cannot explain the feeling."[60]

For most locals, the period between 1989 and 2000 was difficult with few opportunities for work in the villages. After 2004, some people started working in hotels in the developing ski resort Bansko and starting your own business as a guesthouse or a family hotel was perceived as a good opportunity. For most hosts, tourism is not their sole livelihood as the tourist flow is not permanent:

> "It's good, people are interesting, they tell interesting stories. We do also other things, we collect herbs, fruits and mushrooms, dry them, we make tea and different spices, lots of things. And the supermarket is ours, there's a lot of work to do. But we want the guesthouse to be the main business."[61]

One of the most important impacts is of course *the economic benefit:* The unfair distribution of the profits from tourism as well as the exploitation of the local people are another major problem of tourism, when not managed sustainably. According to Nash, the states and large metropolises generating the tourist flow are often those who choose the places to be developed as destinations[62]. When tourism is managed in this way, it is difficult for the local community to serve its own interests, people become victims of exploitation and the economic benefit of tourism development is controversial. This is the case of the ski resort Bansko, where many people from Gorno Draglishte and other villages work in hotels and are in many cases overworked and underpaid. At the same time big all-inclusive hotels in Bansko are undercutting the price of accommodation, driving guesthouses and family hotels out of the market. Bansko used to be a small town in the past but the rapid tourism development in the last twenty years has turned it into the biggest and most popular ski resort in Bulgaria. One of the guesthouse owners in Bansko says:

> "Bansko became a construction site. Big hotels, like barracks. But these are their hotels, the people from the government. They came with their permits and approvals for the construction and our mayor could not do anything. This

is wrong, to give the ski area to people who are not locals. In Austria locals organise themselves. And they all have small hotels, or restaurants, they are responsible for the transportation, the cable car, and the shops. In Austria the concessionaire is the village.[63]

This is why supporting the development of community-based tourism aimed at including locals in decision-making and "empowering" them to create their own business is very important. It is also important to critically analyse and assess whether the work of tourism consulting organisations and NGOs are always in the best interests of the local population.

Even when tourism development is community-based and many members of the community are actively involved in the offering available to tourists, the profit is different for the different stakeholders and there are always stakeholders, who profit more than others do (like guesthouse owners, local pubs and cafés). In the best case these key stakeholders try to distribute the profit by involving other people from the community (e.g. by buying local products, selling local crafts to the tourists or by informing tourists about different services and entertainment offerings, which they otherwise would not be aware of). For instance, the owners of the guesthouse Deshka organise for the tourist groups a visit in a local farm, where they can milk goats and cows and learn how cheese is produced. They also sell different products made by locals (jams, honey, knitted socks, herbs, tea etc.) and try to involve as many women as possible in their folklore programme (traditional dances and songs). *"We sell others people's products, I have no time to prepare these things anyway, but other people… some give me tea, jam, 'shushoni', 'tarlaci' (different types of socks). People want to work but not everybody is used to the contact with tourists"*[64]. Furthermore, the owners always distribute tourists amongst neighbouring guesthouses when they don't have enough free rooms.

However, there are different types of *conflicts within the community caused by competition, jealousy or a clash in the interests* of the different stakeholders. Especially in smaller settlements, the relationships between people profiting from tourism and the rest of the population can change for the worst. According to some of the local hosts, other people are jealous: *"They tell us 'you are not who you used to be, you have become businessmen, it is difficult to talk to you'"*[65].

The relationship between the guesthouse owners and other people changes as the hosts are busy and spend more time with the guests (especially the women): *"I do not have time for such things, they gather here, tattle and gossip, but how can I go with them?"*[66] During the local fair and on big holidays like Easter, Christmas, New Year's Eve, people gather in the local education centre "chitalishte" and celebrate together, occasions on which most of the guesthouse owners are missing. Among the most popular guesthouses (Guesthouse Deshka and Hotel Rudy) there is a strong sense of competition and hostility due to the different way in which they want to present their village and local culture. While Deshka is the defender of the traditional culture (interior of the house, cuisine, folklore programme, dialect), the owners of the hotel Rudy say this is "fake" and it is not how it should be perceived by the visitors. *"We are not like this, our village is modern, one of the few villages* with sewerage … many houses are, we have not lived like this since last century, we do not speak a dialect"[67].

Interestingly these differences only become clear in the individual interviews with the informants, while during the stakeholder workshop all of them shared the same opinions and interests.

Even though the contact is interesting for both sides, communication is difficult because most locals do not speak foreign languages. Tourists speak sometimes English to the children and young people in the families and they try to respond and hold a conversation because they study English at school. Interestingly even though the groups always have a Bulgarian-speaking guide who translates, locals speak directly to the tourists and try to make conversation. In their view, it is very important to communicate with the guests and due to the guides' translation, a big part of the communication gets lost. Sometimes during dinner or during the folklore programme the communication becomes very free and lively. One of the guesthouse owners tells me about the communication with tourists:

> "It is the time to communicate with the guests. And these Australians who came without a guide, we made it somehow. Even the 'Babi' could talk to them, they had no problems, with or without the language, everybody understands, as long as he wants to."[68]

Locals want to learn foreign languages in order to communicate more easily with the tourists:

> "it is our biggest mistake that we do not speak languages"; "people who know foreign languages are great people"; "I want to ask them many things. I am interested in their standard of living. They must be rich. Our country also used to be rich. But now everything has turned upside down!"[69]

According to one of the tourist guides, it is mostly the locals who want to talk to the tourists and start the conversations: "There is always someone who comes and asks 'Where have you been, what did you see, did you like it?'"[70] It is interesting to discuss whether the communication between hosts and guests contributes to improving intercultural communication and overcoming prejudices. In the case of Gorno Draglishte we can see the widely accepted stereotype in Bulgaria of the "western people", who are "unhappy" and "do not know how to have fun and to celebrate":

> "Well, almost all the foreigners I think are very unhappy. That is true. So we try to make them party because I have the feeling that they do not know how to have fun, at least I have this impression. And when we make them party, I look at them and I have the feeling that they've been waiting for such moments for a very long time. As if their faces have completely different expressions. On the next morning they once again have their worried faces. This is how I feel, that they are unhappy, not like us Bulgarians. We are always partying and we are different."[71]

However, the hosts say they can learn many things from communication with the guests and always appreciate their feedback and advice. At the stakeholder workshop the hosts were asked *"Are you worried that contacts with tourists could change you?"*.[72] Most of the answers were that they wanted to change and get to know the western people and their habits and wishes in order to meet their needs. Of course, this can be defined as a form of acculturation, which mainly affects guesthouse owners and their way of life, but cannot affect the entire community.

Other negative impacts on the life of the local community mentioned in literature refer to increased levels of crime, begging, gambling, humiliating local people and increasing levels of (child) prostitution. Burns explains the phenomenon of the "bad" behaviour of some tourists through the so-called "cultural inversion", which occurs in the rules and value system of tourists when they are away from home and "allows" them to do things they would not do at home[73]. Some authors, however, are critical of the role of tourism in increasing crime, prostitution, begging etc. arguing that this is just the "most convenient" explanation for the problems in a given society.

Conclusion

The field study shows the major cultural and socio-economic effects of tourism development, which, due to the manageable number of tourists, mostly impact the people directly involved in tourism and doesn't have a negative impact on the community as a whole.

One of the bigger changes in the villages is the promotion of the region, due to the good media coverage and the growing tourist interest. This leads to a number of other effects, such as a higher self-esteem within the local community regarding natural and cultural assets and triggers awareness on environmental issues. Many of the villagers are keen to get involved in the offering available to tourists but for many of them contact with the tourist industry (tour operators) and the guests is difficult. However, due to the strong tourist flow in some summer and winter seasons, many households welcome guests that cannot be accommodated by existing guesthouses without being official guesthouses themselves. This forms a specific network of actors with some key stakeholders (e.g. guesthouses) who spread the effects of tourism among other members of the community. This influence is mostly perceived as positive by the members of the local community and people are not worried about the cultural changes that may occur, rather they are rather willing to change (learn languages, learn about the habits and needs of tourists).

In terms of cultural change we cannot talk about "damaging the culture" as locals "offer" folklore, traditions, customs and crafts, which otherwise would have disappeared throughout the years. In some cases, the communist regime is mentioned as a cause for abandoning traditions (especially those related to religion and faith), but according to local people this is also due to their desire to adapt to modern society. The return to tradition, folklore and crafts aims to attract and entertain tourists, which in many cases leads to the reinvention of traditions. They already have a different function related to tourism development and economic benefit, and consequently we are talking either about commoditisation or cultural involution. In this case it cannot be argued that tourism "destroys" or "preserves" the culture, as local people are exposed to many other global effects (such as mass media, migration etc.).

Direct contact with guests are perceived as interesting, enjoyable and helpful, and welcoming the guests creates the feeling of festivity and escape from everyday life. This could potentially change with the increasing number of guests and become a routine service without a personal touch. Given the example of Bansko, another potential change could stem from attracting foreign investment, which would turn tourism into a kind of imperialism and often does not even guarantee jobs for the locals. From the development of tourism in Bansko we can conclude that it is not the tourists themselves, but rather the local or foreign entrepreneurs that are the agents of change as they manage the supply, the demand and the flow of tourists. This is also true for the villages of Gorno Draglishte and Dobarsko, where the established local stakeholders, as well as tourist companies and consultants contribute to the development of tourism. It could be said that the changes due to tourism at this stage are rather internal and not so much due to the external influence of the tourists that arrive in the village. However, in the case of Gorno Draglishte and Dobarsko there no strong negative consequences have stemmed from the development of tourism. Tourism has actually developed strongly over the past ten years, but has not reached the critical point where major negative changes would taking place. This is largely due to the fact that the villages are not yet the subject of mass tourism, and local stakeholders and tourism companies, which organise tours in the region, are monitoring and managing the influence they have on the local community.

Notes

1 Stronza, Amanda (2001): *Anthropology of Tourism: Forging New Ground for Ecotourism and Other Alternatives.* In: Annual Review of Anthropology, Vol. 30, pp. 261–283, p. 264.
2 Cf. Nash, Dennison/Smith, Valene L. (1991): *Anthropology and tourism.* In: Annals of Tourism Research, Vol. 18, pp. 12–25.
3 Cf. Burns, Peter (1999): *An Introduction to Tourism and Anthropology.* London: Routledge.
4 Cf. Nash, Dennison (1996): *The Anthropology of Tourism.* Bingley (UK): Emerald.
5 MacCannell, Dean (1976): *The Tourist: A New Theory of the Leisure Class.* Berkeley/Los Angeles: University of California Press, p. 91.
6 Cf. Nash (1996): *The Anthropology of Tourism*; Urry, John (1990): *The Tourist Gaze: Leisure and Travel in Contemporary Societies.* London/Newbury Park: Sage Publications.
7 Cf. MacCannell (1976): *The Tourist*, pp. 91–95.
8 Burns (1999): *An Introduction to Tourism and Anthropology*, p. 71.
9 Stronza (2001): *Anthropology of Tourism*, p. 274.
10 United Nations Environment Programme (UNEP)/World Tourism Organization (WTO) (2005): *Making Tourism More Sustainable. A Guide for Policy Makers*, p. 11. Available from: http://www.unep.fr/shared/publications/pdf/dtix0592xpa-tourismpolicyen.pdf [01.05.2012].

11 Ibid.

12 Cf. Goodwin, Harold (2006): *Measuring and Reporting the Impact of Tourism on Poverty*. Paper presented at the Cutting Edge Research in Tourism New Directions, Challenges and Applications, 6–9 June 2006, School of Management, University of Surrey, UK. Available from: http://www.haroldgoodwin.info/resources/measuring.pdf [01.05.2012].

13 Cf. Smith, Valene L. (1989, ed.): *Hosts and Guests: The Anthropology of Tourism*. 2nd ed. Philadelphia: University of Pennsylvania Press; Burns (1999): *An Introduction to Tourism and Anthropology*.

14 After Smith (1989): *Hosts and Guests*, pp. 12–15.

15 Ibid.

16 Cf. Krippendorf, Jost (2011): *The Holiday Makers: Understanding the Impact of Leisure and Travel*. New York: Routledge.

17 Cf. Mathieson, Alister/Wall, Geoffrey (2006): *Tourism: Change, Impacts and Opportunities*. London: Pearson Education Limited.

18 Cf. Burns (1999): *An Introduction to Tourism and Anthropology*, p. 102.

19 Cf. Wood, Robert E. (1993): *Tourism, Culture, and the Sociology of Development*. In: Hitchcock, Michael/King, Viktor T./Parnwall, Mike (eds): *Tourism in South-East Asia*. London: Routledge, pp. 48–70.

20 Byrd, Erick T. (2007): *Stakeholders in sustainable tourism development and their roles: applying stakeholder theory to sustainable tourism development*. In: Tourism Review, Vol. 62 (2), pp. 6–13, p. 7.

21 Cf. Burns (1999): *An Introduction to Tourism and Anthropology*; Nunez, Theron/Lett, James (1989): *Touristic Studies in Anthropological Perspective*. In: Smith, Valene L. (ed.): Hosts and Guests: The Anthropology of Tourism. 2nd ed. Philadelphia: University of Pennsylvania Press, pp. 263–280.

22 Cf. Nash (1996): *The Anthropology of Tourism*.

23 Burns (1999): *An Introduction to Tourism and Anthropology*.

24 Ibid., p. 101.

25 Ibid.

26 Cf. Burns (1999): *An Introduction to Tourism and Anthropology*.

27 MacCannell (1976): *The Tourist*, p. 91.

28 Cf. MacCannell, Dean (1992): *Empty Meeting Grounds. The Tourist Papers*. New York: Routledge, pp. 17–74.

29 Mowforth, Martin/Munt, Ian (2009): *Tourism and Sustainability: Development, Globalization and New Tourism in the Third World*. 3rd ed. London/New York: Routledge, p. 261.

30 Wood, Robert E. (1997): *Tourism and the State: Ethnic Options and Constructions of Otherness*. In: Picard, Michel/Wood, Robert E. (eds.): Tourism, ethnicity and the state in Asian and Pacific Societies. Honolulu: University of Hawai'i Press, pp. 1–34, p. 8.

31 Cf. Krippendorf (1987): *The Holiday Makers*, pp. 106–108.

32 Katelieva, Maria (2012): *Field Notes* [unpublished], Gorno Draglishte, Dobarsko, April–May 2012.

33 Ibid.

34 Ibid.

35 Ibid.

36 Cf. Hobsbawm, Eric (1983): *The Invention of Tradition*. Cambridge/New York: Cambridge University Press.

37 Cf. de Botton, Alan (2002): *The Art of Travel*. New York: Vintage Books.

38 Cf. *Cape Town Declaration on Responsible Tourism*. Available from: http://responsibletourismpartnership.org/cape-town-declaration-on-responsible-tourism/ [01.05.2012].

39 McKean, Philip Frick (1989): *Towards a Theoretical Analysis of Tourism: Economic Dualism and Cultural Involution in Bali*. In: Smith, Valene L. (ed.): Hosts and Guests: The Anthropology of Tourism. 2nd ed. Philadelphia: University of Pennsylvania Press, pp. 119–138, pp. 125–126.

40 Ibid.

41 Shepherd, Robert (2002): *Commodification, culture and tourism*. In: Tourist Studies, Vol. 2 (2), pp. 183–201, p. 185.

42 Kasfir, Sidney L. (1999): *Samburu Souvenirs: Representations of a Land in Amber*. In: Phillips, Ruth B./Steiner, Christopher B. (eds.): Unpacking Culture. Art and Commodity in Colonial and Postcolonial Worlds. Berkeley: University of California, pp. 67–86, p. 79.

43 Ibid., p. 81.

44 Katelieva (2012): *Field Notes*.

45 Ibid.

46 Cf. Boissevain, Jeremy (1996): *Coping with Tourists. European Reactions to Mass Tourism*. Providence/Oxford: Berghahn Books, p. 6.

47 Cf. Burns (1999): *An Introduction to Tourism and Anthropology*.

48 Katelieva (2012): *Field Notes*.

49 Ibid.

50 Cf. Smith (1989): *Hosts and Guests*; Phillips, Ruth B./Steiner, Christopher B. (1999, eds.): *Unpacking Culture. Art and Commodity in Colonial and Postcolonial Worlds*. Berkeley: University of California.

51 Cf. Boissevain (1996): *Coping with Tourists*, pp. 13–14.

52 Katelieva, Maria (2012): *Field Notes*.

53 Ibid.

54 Ibid.

55 Cf. MacCannell (1976): *The Tourist*, pp. 91–95.

56 Graburn, Nelson H. H. (1999). *Epilogue: Ethnic and Tourist Arts revisited*. In: Phillips, Ruth B./Steiner, Christopher B. (eds.): Unpacking Culture, pp. 335–354, p. 350.

57 Cf. MacCannell (1976). *The Tourist*, pp. 92–95.

58 Cf. Boissevain (1996): *Coping with Tourists*, p. 14.

59 Katelieva, Maria (2012): *Field Notes*.

60 Ibid.

61 Ibid.

62 Cf. Nash (1996): The Anthropology of Tourism, pp. 59–79.

63 Katelieva, Maria (2012): *Field Notes*.

64 Ibid.

65 Ibid.

66 Ibid.

67 Ibid.

68 Ibid.

69 Ibid.

70 Ibid.

71 Ibid.

72 Ibid.

73 Cf. Burns (1999): *An Introduction to Tourism and Anthropology*, p. 86.

III Städte im Wandel.
Entwicklung und
Nachhaltigkeit der Städte im
globalen Süden –

Kurzfassungen von
Einreichungen zum
Entwicklungsforschungspreis
2015

Johannes Knierzinger

Unternehmerische Kontrolle in guineischen Bauxitstädten: Wie man von einem Löwen springt

Ich habe mich in den letzten vier Jahren mit den soziopolitischen Konsequenzen von Bauxitabbau in Guinea beschäftigt. In dieser Zusammenfassung werde ich versuchen, die Ergebnisse dieser Recherchen in Bezug auf die Fragestellungen in der Ausschreibung zu präsentieren. Weitere Analyseabschnitte befinden sich in den Kapiteln 3.3 und 4 der publizierten Version meiner Dissertation[1].

Guinea ist einer der ressourcenreichsten Staaten der Erde – verfügt über die weltweit größten Bauxitvorkommen, die größte Eisenerzlagerstätte, umfangreiche Goldvorkommen und ein vielzitiertes Potential für Wasserkraft – rangiert jedoch gleichzeitig unter den letzten Staaten im Human Development Index und zählt laut Oxfam zu den Ländern mit den höchsten Nahrungsmittelpreisen (relativ zum Einkommen). Die Gründe für dieses „paradox of plenty" sind vielfältig: Der Export von Rohstoffen (bis heute überwiegend nach Europa) führt zur Entwicklung von Enklaven, fördert Korruption und hat schwerwiegende demokratiepolitische Konsequenzen. Ich konzentrierte mich vor allem auf den letzten Punkt und untersuchte dazu die politischen Konsequenzen von Bauxitabbau in den vier guineischen Bauxitstädten in Sangaredi, Kamsar, Fria und Débélé/Kindia (siehe Abbildung 1). Die dominierenden Forschungsfragen stehen in engem Zusammenhang mit dem zweiten Fragekomplex der Ausschreibung:

Vor welchen sozialen, technologischen, architektonischen, raumplanerischen, kulturellen, infrastrukturellen etc. Herausforderungen stehen Städte im globalen Süden und was kann die Entwicklungsforschung zu der Bewältigung dieser spezifischen Probleme beitragen?

Es ging mir insbesondere um Machtverhältnisse und Möglichkeiten der politischen Partizipation in diesen Städten. Dazu unternahm ich eine umfangreiche Literaturrecherche zur Geschichte Guineas und der globalen Aluminiumproduktion und verbrachte fünf Monate in den Bauxitstädten, um den Alltag in den Arbeiterhaushalten, Bauxitminen und angrenzenden Dörfern kennen zu lernen. Während dieses Aufenthalts führte ich 150 halbstrukturierte Interviews mit allen beteiligten AkteurInnen durch und stellte kleinere Studien zur Ernährungssituation, zur Bildung und zur Lohnentwicklung in den Städten an. Die anleitenden theoretischen Konzepte zur Untersuchung dieser Städte entwickelte ich vor allem aus Ansätzen der Globalen Güterkettenforschung[2].

Bauxit wird für die Aluminiumerzeugung verwendet und war von der frühen guineischen Unabhängigkeit 1958 bis in die späten 1990er die fast ausschließliche Quelle des guineischen Regierungsbudgets. Diese Minenstädte mit gegenwärtig nicht mehr als insgesamt 10.000 direkt Beschäftigten prägten damit die gesamte Geschichte Guineas: Sowohl die wenigen direkt Angestellten als auch die ausländischen Minenkonzerne verfügen bis heute über ein großes Erpressungspotential gegenüber der guineischen Regierung. Die Minenstädte selbst wurden von meinen InterviewpartnerInnen immer wieder als Mikrogesellschaften bezeichnet: Mangels existierender Infrastruktur und auch um ausländische Arbeitskräfte anzuziehen, bauten die beteiligten Konzerne (u. a. aus Frankreich, den USA, Kanada, der Sowjetunion und Deutschland) fast im Alleingang ganze Städte – von Wohnungen, Elektrizitätswerken, Wasseraufbereitungsanlagen, Spitälern, Straßen und Zugverbindungen bis hin zu halböffentlichen Swimmingpools, Fußballstadien, Kirchen und Leichenhallen. Die ArbeiterInnen und in vielen Fällen auch Teile der restlichen Bevölkerung (in drei der vier Städte etwas mehr als 100.000 EinwohnerInnen) hatten Zugang zu guter medizinischer Versorgung, kostenlosem Strom, Trinkwasser, Abfallentsorgung, relativ guten Bildungssystemen und die Konzerne kontrollierten weite Teile der Sicherheitskräfte und der lokalen Medien.

Abbildung 1: Übersichtskarte Guineas³

Nach einer Rohstoffhausse bis in die 1970er änderte sich diese Situation jedoch und die politischen Langzeitfolgen dieser Machtkonstellation wurden sichtbar: Die Konzerne begannen zu sparen – zuerst bei der Bevölkerung die nicht direkt angestellt war und dann auch bei den Arbeiterfamilien – und die Bevölkerung wurde sich bewusst, dass sie nur wenige Mittel hatte, um etwas dagegen zu tun. Die Finanzierung und Aufrechterhaltung der Städte durch die Konzerne war nur ungenügend durch Gesetzte abgesichert. Im April 2012 führten Arbeiterproteste und kontinuierliche Zusammenstöße zwischen Sicherheitskräften und der Bevölkerung in Fria vor diesem Hintergrund schließlich zu einem „Lock-out": Der Aluminiumkonzern Rusal verriegelte seine Bauxitfabrik und zog sein russisches Personal ab, ohne den Status der guineischen ArbeiterInnen zu klären, zahlte keine Löhne mehr aus und garantierte nur eine minimale Versorgung der Stadt mit Strom, Wasser und anderen Dienstleistungen wie etwa medizinischer Betreuung. Der Konzern profitiert von dieser Lage eindeutig: Auch ohne diesen Konflikt wäre er aufgrund der schlechten konjunkturellen Lage gezwungen gewesen, die Produktion in diesem oder anderen Betrieben stillzulegen – in diesem Fall hätte er jedoch die ArbeiterInnen während dieser Phase bezahlen, mit Strom und Wasser versorgen und medizinische Betreuung sicherstellen müssen. Meine Recherchen ergaben, dass das Nichtausbezahlen der Löhne in weiten Teilen der Bevölkerung Frias zu Unterernährung führte. Eine weitere guineische Minenstadt, Débélé, könnte in den nächsten Jahren geschlossen werden, weil kein abbauwürdiger Bauxit mehr vorhanden ist. Ihrer Bevölkerung steht ein ähnliches Schicksal bevor, wenn auch auf geringerem Niveau: Die Stadt ist kleiner und befindet sich in der Nähe einer größeren Stadt. Bisher wurden aber auch in diesem Fall keine Vorkehrungen für die Situation nach dem Abzug des Bergbaukonzerns getroffen.

Wie lassen sich partizipative, menschenadäquate urbane Konzepte vor dem Hintergrund anhaltender Stadtmigration realisieren?

In der Conclusio der Dissertation und in den Kapiteln zu den einzelnen Minenstädten versuche ich zu klären, wie solche Situationen extremer Abhängigkeit vermieden oder abgefedert werden können. Vor allem die Frage der politischen Partizipation in diesen stark wachsenden Städten erhält bisher wenig Aufmerksamkeit, weder in der Literatur noch in der entwicklungspolitischen Praxis. Ein detaillierter Vergleich des Budgets der Stadtverwaltung von Kamsar mit den Budgets der Bergbaukonzerne, die in öffentlich genutzte Infrastruktur und öffentliche Dienstleistungen fließen, hat etwa gezeigt, dass der Stadtgemeinderat weniger als ein Prozent dieser Investitionen kontrolliert. Abgesehen von der Bezahlung der Beamten werden auch von staatlicher Seite praktisch keine Investitionen getätigt. Wahlen haben in diesem Kontext nur eine geringe Bedeutung, weil die gewählten Repräsentanten nur über wenig bestimmen können. Auf lange Frist entstand dadurch eine Hinwendung zum Konzern als politischem Entscheidungsträger und dieser scheint diese Position auch in immer stärkerem Maße zu akzeptieren. Die auch im Bergbausektor immer stärker präsenten Maßnahmen der sozialen Unternehmensverantwortung *(Corporate Social Responsibility)* scheinen diese Entwicklung noch zu verstärken. Meine Untersuchungen haben gezeigt, dass Effizienz und Partizipation im Rahmen solcher sozialer Maßnahmen als Gegensatz verstanden werden: Den CSR-Verantwortlichen innerhalb der Konzerne zufolge verschwinden umso mehr Gelder in privaten Taschen, je stärker die Regionalverwaltung und andere lokale Gruppen einbezogen werden. Aus Angst vor Sanktionen durch die ohnehin spärlichen internationalen Kontrollinstanzen (z. B. über die *Environmental and Social Performance Standards* der *International Finance Corporation*) lehnen diese Entscheidungsträger etwa budgetäre Partizipationsmöglichkeiten ab und sprechen sich gegen demokratische Mechanismen bei der Vergabe von Jobs aus. Die Auswahl der Projekte basiert auf einem elaborierten Entscheidungsfindungsprozess, der theoretisch auf Dorfebene startet. In der Praxis werden die meisten Entscheidungen jedoch auf Firmenebene getroffen und in Streitfällen hat der Konzern in jedem Fall das letzte Wort. Das Ergebnis ist eine generelle Entwicklung der Städte, die den Interessen der Bergbaukonzerne folgt und de facto ein despotisches politisches System etabliert: Die Bevölkerung muss sich den Entscheidungen einer strikt hierarchisch organisierten, privatwirtschaftlichen Kommandokette, von den Investoren über die Minendirektoren bis hin zu den CSR-Verantwortlichen und den technischen Verantwortlichen vor Ort, fügen.

Ein Gutteil der Dissertation zielt dementsprechend darauf ab zu zeigen, dass der demokratiepolitische Handlungsspielraum in diesen Minenstädten sehr begrenzt ist und dass demokratischer Druck aus den Herkunftsstaaten der Minenkonzerne – etwa durch die Verankerung von lokaler Partizipation und sozialen Mindeststandards in bilateralen Handelsverträgen[4] – unumgänglich ist. Auf nationaler Ebene wurden solche Klauseln auch mit der Neufassung der Minengesetzgebung 2012 beschlossen, aber aufgrund ihrer unklaren Formulierung bisher nicht umgesetzt. Auf Städteebene wird weiterhin lokaler Druck auf die Konzerne ausgeübt, ihre Unternehmensverantwortung auch in Bezug auf langfristige politische Verantwortung wahrzunehmen. Einige dahingehende Ansätze sind in zwei Goldbergbaustädten Guineas sichtbar, wo die Stadtverwaltung zumindest kleine Teile der Investitionen von öffentlichem Interesse in der Form von Lokalsteuern kontrolliert. Weitere abfedernde Maßnahmen wären Capacity-Building-Programme, die auf die Zeit nach dem Bauxitbergbau abzielen, wie etwa effektivere Subsistenzwirtschaft oder der Anbau von *cash crops*. Die klassische Entwicklungszusammenarbeit hat sich von den Firmenstädten bisher überwiegend ferngehalten, mit dem Argument, dass von Firmenseite bereits genug investiert wird – mit den beschriebenen Konsequenzen.

In welcher Wechselwirkung – und damit in welchem Problemkontext – stehen rurale Gebiete und wachsende Städte im globalen Süden?

In allen vier guineischen Bauxitstädten kam es in den letzten Jahren zu Konflikten, die einerseits generell aus politischer Frustration, andererseits aber auch aus den großen Disparitäten zwischen den EinwohnerInnen resultieren. Alle vier Städte können in einen von Arbeiterfamilien dominierten Stadtkern und eine benachteiligte Peripherie, bestehend aus einer steigenden Zahl von indirekt Beschäftigten, Gelegenheitsarbeitskräften, HandwerkerInnen, DienstleisterInnen und BäuerInnen, eingeteilt werden. Vormals in der Region existierende Machtverhältnisse (beruhend auf Alter, Religion, Gender, „traditionellen" Herrschaftsformen etc.) wurden durch die *relativ* hohen Arbeiterlöhne und die Infrastrukturmacht[5] der Konzerne grundlegend verändert. Doch dieser „Stadtkern" hat auch zeitliche Grenzen. Ein großer Teil der ArbeiterInnen verbringt den Lebensabend in Armut: Die staatliche Pension ist vernachlässigbar und Ansprüche auf Gratiswohnungen, medizinische Versorgung und verbilligte Nahrungsmittel gehen mit der Pensionierung verloren. Das führt dazu, dass ganze Arbeiterfamilien mit 20 bis 30 Mitgliedern bei der Pensionierung einer einzigen ArbeiterIn in die Armut gestürzt werden. Männliche Arbeiter haben in der Regel zwei bis drei Frauen und nehmen dazu auch noch Kinder von entfernen Verwandten in den Haushalt auf.

Die durchwegs auf Subsistenz angewiesene Bevölkerung in der Nähe der Minen ist die einzige betroffene Bevölkerungsgruppe, die von einem Ende des Bauxitabbaus unmittelbar profitieren würde (langfristig würden mit großer Sicherheit der Großteil der StädterInnen und AnrainerInnen profitieren): Trotz eines sich zaghaft durchsetzenden Nachhaltigkeitsdiskurses innerhalb und außerhalb der Bergbaukonzerne werden ihre Felder weiterhin durch Tagebauminen zerstört, Flussläufe und Brunnen trocknen aufgrund von Sprengungen aus und die Staubbelastung führt zu Erkrankungen der Atemwege und der Augen. Meinen Recherchen zufolge waren Umsiedlungsprogramme bisher in keinem einzigen Fall erfolgreich und auch die Entschädigungsmaßnahmen entsprachen in keinem analysierten Fall dem zerstörten Sachwert. Die betroffene Bevölkerung besteht fast ausschließlich aus AnalphabetInnen und kann deshalb die existierenden Beschwerdemechanismen nicht nutzen. Die verantwortlichen Beamten verfügen nicht über die Mittel (kein Geld, um Benzin zu kaufen und in vielen Fällen auch über kein Motorrad), um Lokalaugenscheine durchzuführen. Dieses Machtgefälle zwischen Stadt- und Landbevölkerung hat sich entgegen meinen Erwartungen auch während der Krise in Fria nicht geändert, etwa durch die Versorgung der Stadtbevölkerung mit Reis aus dem Umland. Dazu war die landwirtschaftliche Produktivität zu gering und das kulturelle und soziale Kapital der ehemaligen Arbeiterfamilien zu hoch. Andere Kräfteverhältnisse haben sich jedoch grundlegend verändert: Frauen übernahmen im Laufe der Krise mehr und mehr politische Funktionen, offiziell wie auch im Alltag, und auch religiöse Führer traten wieder verstärkt als Vermittler auf.

Weitere Konflikte in den Minenstädten betreffen Pensionierungen (die Gewerkschaften kämpfen geschlossen für eine *Anhebung* des Pensionsalters), Strom- und Trinkwasserversorgung, die Abfallentsorgung und andere ökologische Probleme, wie etwa die Verunreinigung des Grundwassers und die Versorgung der ArbeiterInnen und von Teilen der Bevölkerung mit verbilligten Nahrungsmitteln aus dem Ausland (z. B. Reis aus den USA und Zucker aus Österreich).

Sind Resilienz und Nachhaltigkeit bloß Schlagwörter, die kaum eine Entsprechung in der urbanen Realität von morgen finden werden?

Die guineischen Bauxitstädte sind Teil eines globalen Netzwerks von (konkurrierenden) Städten, die über ein relativ konsolidiertes Produktionsnetzwerk miteinander verbunden sind. Aufgrund hoher Steuererleichterungen und Subventionen befinden sich die meisten Verarbeitungsbetriebe von guineischem Bauxit immer noch in Europa, etwa im norddeutschen Stade oder im irischen Aughinish. Auch diese Städte sind in großem Ausmaß auf das Produktionsnetzwerk des globalen Aluminiumoligopols angewiesen.

Ökologische und soziale Nachhaltigkeit in diesen Städten hängt dementsprechend vor allem von einer Demokratisierung globalisierter Produktionsstrukturen ab, was kein leichtes Unterfangen ist. Aluminium war bis in die 1960er ein Kriegsrohstoff (v. a. für Flugzeuge) und bleibt bis heute ein wesentlicher Faktor geopolitischer Strategien. Eine generelle Reduktion der Produktion scheint aus heutiger Sicht unumgänglich: Aluminiumschmelzen verbrauchen so viel Energie wie fast kein anderer Industriebetrieb, gleichzeitig wird das Metall aber in großem Umfang für Verpackungen und Getränkedosen eingesetzt. In diesem Zusammenhang entstand vor Kurzem auch eine Diskussion über gesundheitlich bedenkliche Produkte aus Aluminium[6]. Im Sinne einer produktionskettenübergreifenden Solidarität – von Protesten gegen guineische Bauxitminen und gegen die Verunreinigung von Gewässern durch Rotschlamm (dem Abfallprodukt bei der Bauxitraffination), bis hin zu Verbraucheraktionen gegen die Verwendung von Aluminium in Deodorants oder Kaffeemaschinen – geht es also vor allem um eine Reduktion der Produktion durch Abfallvermeidung, Recycling und die Suche nach alternativen Rohstoffen.

Die Situation in Guinea offenbart aber auch produktionskettenübergreifende Machtkonstellationen, die im Stande sind, demokratische Entscheidungsfindung in einem bedeutend höheren Ausmaß auszuhebeln. In meiner Dissertation nenne ich unter anderem Fria als ein konkretes Beispiel dafür. Die Misere in der Firmenstadt hätte durch eine weniger risikobehaftete Investitionspolitik des Konzerns vor der Subprime-Krise mit großer Wahrscheinlichkeit verhindert werden können. Das Problem ist aber nun nicht so sehr diese Fehlentscheidung eines einzelnen Investors, sondern der Umstand, dass eine solche Fehlentscheidung zu derartigen Konsequenzen führen kann. Dieses demokratiepolitische Problem ist meiner Ansicht nach die größte „globale Herausforderung" der gegenwärtigen Entwicklungspolitik.

Zu diesem Zweck müssen Medienkampagnen zu den Konsequenzen globalisierter industrieller Produktion weiterhin mit der Erarbeitung rechtlicher Rahmenbedingungen für global agierende Konzerne – wie zuletzt etwa mit dem *Dodd-Frank Act* oder der *Extractive Industries Transparency Initiative* – kombiniert werden[7]. Die seit drei Jahren skandalöse Lage in Fria ist immer noch nicht in deutschsprachige Medien vorgedrungen. Würde es sich in Fria um die Produktion von Smartphones handeln, so wäre wahrscheinlich schon genug öffentlicher Druck für eine einvernehmliche Lösung entstanden. Die etwas verschlungeneren Wege von Bauxit in die Haushalte des globalen Nordens und das Fehlen bewaffneter Konflikte scheinen aber bisher einer medialen Berichterstattung in deutsch- und englischsprachigen Ländern entgegenzuwirken.

Das politische und wirtschaftliche Vakuum in Fria wurde in der Zwischenzeit durch zahlreiche Initiativen der lokalen Zivilgesellschaft gefüllt, die auf eine Zukunft ohne Minen abzielen und die Stadt durch Tourismus, nachhaltige Landwirtschaft und Bildungsprojekte wieder lebenswerter gestalten wollen. Entwicklungspolitische Projekte könnten bei diesen vielversprechenden Beispielen anknüpfen, um auf die beschriebenen größeren Zusammenhänge zu verweisen.

Anmerkungen

1 Knierzinger, Johannes (2017): *Bauxite Mining in Africa. Transnational Corporate Governance and Development*. Basingstoke: Palgrave Macmillan. Online unter: https://books.google.fr/books/about/Bauxite_Mining_in_Africa.html?id=Jq80DwAAQBAJ&redir_esc=y.

2 Vgl. Bair, Jennifer (2009, Hrsg.): *Frontiers of commodity chain research*. Stanford: Stanford University Press.

3 CIA World Factbook (2015): *Topographic map of Guinea*. Online unter: https://commons.wikimedia.org/wiki/File:Guinea_Physiography.jpg [05.05.2018].

4 Vgl. Küblböck, Karin (2014): *Can "Undistorted Access" Lead to Inclusive Development? The EU Raw Materials Initiative and Possible Effects upon Resource-Based Development in Africa*. In: Journal für Entwicklungspolitik 30 (3), S. 89–105.

5 Vgl. Agnew, John (2005): *Sovereignty Regimes: Territoriality and State Authority in Contemporary World Politics*. In: Annals of the Association of American Geographers, 95 (2), S. 437–461.

6 Vgl. z. B. ORF (2015): *Bundesheer verbannt Aluminiumgeschirr*. Online unter: http://orf.at/stories/2269610/2269611/ [08.07.2015].

7 Vgl. z. B. Lukas, Karin/Plank, Leonhard/Staritz, Cornelia (2009): *Securing Labour Rights in Global Production Networks. Legal Instruments and Policy Options*. Wien: Arbeiterkammer Wien.

Robert Hafner

handlung | macht | raum

Urbane Materialsammler-Kooperativen und ihre
Livelihoods-Strategien in Buenos Aires

In Buenos Aires fallen täglich mehr als 5000 Tonnen Müll an. Materialsammler, jene, die ihren Lebensunterhalt mit dem Abfall der Gesellschaft verdienen, blieben bis zur Wirtschaftskrise 2001 in Argentinien in vollkommener Unsichtbarkeit. Erst durch den rapiden Anstieg dieser informellen und marginalisierten Gruppe und ihr vermehrtes Auftreten im öffentlichen Raum wurde ihre Existenz wahrgenommen.

Die Thematik der Abfallwirtschaft führt wie kaum eine andere in die „informelle Stadt", in der sich die Frage nach Zugangs- und Verfügungsrechten permanent stellt und wo die Bedingungen der Überlebenssicherung sowie die Möglichkeiten und Grenzen der Aneignung städtischen Raumes immer wieder ausgehandelt werden. Vor diesem Hintergrund setzt sich dieses Buch eingehend mit dem Ansatz der Politischen Ökologie, der für die Arbeit erkenntnisleitend ist, auseinander. Ergänzt wird dies dabei durch grundlegende Überlegungen zu Handlung, Macht und Raum. Hierbei wird nicht nur auf die in der jüngeren Sozialgeographie zum Thema entstandenen Arbeiten zurückgegriffen, sondern auch Grundlegendes aus den Nachbardisziplinen, aus der Soziologie und Philosophie eingeflochten. Giddens' Verständnis von Handlung und Macht, wie auch grundsätzliche Überlegungen von Foucault und Bourdieu setzen den Rahmen für die tiefgreifende empirische Aufarbeitung.

Wurde das Thema der informellen Müllsammler in anderen Städten, wie Kairo, São Paulo, oder Delhi bereits intensiv behandelt, so waren die *cirujas*, wie die informellen Materialsammler in Buenos Aires genannt wurden, sowohl im öffentlichen Bewusstsein als auch in der sozialwissenschaftlichen Forschung lange Zeit wenig präsent. Bereits im 19. Jahrhundert verfolgten die Stadtregierungen eine Politik der Segregation in einen sozio-ökonomisch bevorzugten, von Abfall befreiten Norden und einen dreckigen, mit Krankheiten und Mülldeponien verseuchten südlichen Teil der Stadt. Der Aktions- und Lebensradius der Müllsammler beschränkte sich auf die stets wachsenden Slums und die umliegenden Müllhalden; die Lebensbedingungen blieben weitgehend unsichtbar für die dominierende Gesellschaft. Dies änderte sich in den 1990er Jahren schlagartig: Eine neoliberale Politik um jeden Preis führte dazu, dass immer mehr Menschen ihre Arbeit verloren und im informellen (Abfall-)Sektor ihre einzige Verdienstmöglichkeit sahen. Abfallsammeln wurde mehr und mehr zu einer der Überlebensstrategien, insbesondere an der

Spitze der Wirtschaftskrise 2000/2001, sodass bis zu 100.000 – nun als *cartoneros* bezeichnete – Materialsammler die Stadt überfluteten. Besonders der traditionell bevorzugte Norden der Stadt eignete sich – aufgrund der gut ausgebauten ÖPNV-Infrastruktur – gut für die neuen Tätigkeiten. Eine weitere Besonderheit ist, dass die *cartoneros* der Krise ein Gesicht gaben, durchaus anerkennend konnotiert mit dem Ausspruch *„pobres pero dignos"* – „arm aber mit Würde"; ein fundamentaler Baustein für die Transformation eines informellen Sektors in Richtung Formalisierung.

Basierend auf diesem – bereits auch medial gut dokumentierten – Kontext präsentiert das vorliegende Buch einen neuen Fokus, der das ohnehin komplexe Spannungsfeld zwischen Informalität und Formalität in neuem Licht präsentiert. Zehn Jahre nach der eigentlichen Krise haben sich die Organisationsformen und Grundstrukturen der städtischen Materialsammlung grundlegend verändert. Seit Mitte des vergangenen Jahrzehnts geht es um die Formalisierung der bisher ausschließlich informellen Aktivität. Die Materialsammler-Kooperativen bilden jetzt offiziell einen festen Bestandteil der Abfallwirtschaft, zuständig für die wiederverwertbaren Materialen. Mit der Möglichkeit der Kooperativenbildung tritt ein spannendes Element auf: Es wird nicht mehr von *den* Materialsammlern gesprochen, es entwickeln sich hoch diversifizierte Überlebensstrategien, die stark durch persönliche Biografien, soziales Umfeld und Denkweise der Kooperativenmitglieder geprägt sind. Ebendiese Strategien werden am Beispiel von vier Kooperativen visualisiert. Es werden die vielfältigen Verflechtungen und Einflüsse, die zwischen der formellen und der informellen Seite der Stadt bestehen, aufgezeigt. Auf der Basis von Interviews und (zumeist teilnehmender) Beobachtungen, sozusagen „aus erster Hand" wird eine differenzierte „Innensicht" auf die Alltagspraktiken, lebensweltlichen Problemstellungen, Handlungslogiken und -konflikten herausgearbeitet. Räumliche Praktiken, Organisationsstrukturen und Ideologien stehen dabei genauso im Vordergrund, wie auch Interaktionen und Handlungen mit und Machtverhältnisse zwischen den beteiligten Akteuren im sozialen Raum.

Dabei zeigt sich sehr deutlich, dass Sichtbarkeit auf unterschiedlichen Ebenen (nachbarschaftlich, zwischen verschiedenen Kooperativen, zwischen Kooperativen und der Stadtregierung, wie auch zu internationalen Organisationen), von fundamentaler Bedeutung für die Kooperativen ist. Die Kooperative *DEL OESTE* besteht aus Handwerkern, die während der Krise 2000/2001 ihre Arbeit verloren. Ihren Fokus legen sie rein auf die Arbeit des Trennens und wollen auf sämtlichen Ebenen unsichtbar bleiben. Die Kooperative zeichnet das Bild eines traditionell geführten Kleinbetriebes, jedoch mit großen Problemen bei der Durchsetzung von eigenen Interessen gegenüber anderen Kooperativen und der Stadtregierung. *El CorreCamino*, eine quasi-anarchische Gruppe mit stark informellem Hintergrund, setzt ihren Fokus auf die Nachbarschaft, ist dort gut verankert und sieht ihre Stärke in der Unsichtbarkeit. Sie bezeichnen sich mittlerweile selbst als *promotores ambientales*, als Umweltpromotoren. *El Ceibo*, die dritte Kooperative, setzt stark auf internationales Marketing und Kooperationen mit Nichtregierungsorganisationen, um so ihr Überleben zu sichern. Die vierte Gruppe, *Amanecer (MTE)* sieht sich selbst als soziale Bewegung, denn eine Kooperative zählt auf die Anzahl ihrer Mitglieder (über 2.500, im Vergleich zu ca. 10–80 der anderen Kooperativen), verfügt über eine kritische Masse und kann so ihre Forderungen, insbesondere gegenüber der Stadtregierung, erfolgreich durchsetzen.

Die vier unterschiedlichen Strategien von Materialsammlerkooperativen zeigen sehr deutlich, dass Abfallwirtschaft in Buenos Aires zwar widerwillig aber endgültig ihren Platz auf der politischen Agenda gefunden hat. Die stark divergierenden Denk- und Handlungsweisen der Kooperativen stellen nun jedoch nicht nur die Zivilbevölkerung, sondern auch die Stadt- und nationale Politik, ebenso wie internationale Entscheidungsträger vor die Herausforderung, einen adäquaten Umgang mit daraus resultierenden neuen raumbezogenen Konflikten und Machtbeziehungen im Bereich der Abfallwirtschaft zu finden. Dieses Buch soll durch einen neuen, einen Blick von Innen, einen ersten Schritt dazu leisten.

Elisabeth Huber

Über das Potential der „Armen" in westafrikanischen Städten, umweltgerecht zu handeln

Auf der Grundlage von theoretischen Überlegungen und einer empirischen Erhebung befasst sich diese Doktorarbeit mit Armut und ihren Auswirkungen auf umweltgerechtes Handeln im urbanen Raum in Westafrika. In einem Zeitraum von insgesamt über zwölf Monaten wurde eine ethnographische Forschung in Bamako (Mali) in den Jahren 2011 und 2012 sowie in Ouagadougou (Burkina Faso) in den Jahren 2013 und 2014 durchgeführt. Die Forschungsfrage thematisiert die Möglichkeiten, welche ärmeren städtischen Bevölkerungsschichten gegeben sind, um umweltgerecht zu handeln. Die Praktiken der Abfall- und Abwasserentsorgung werden unter den dafür relevanten ökonomischen, sozialen und kulturellen Bedingungen analysiert. Aus einer anthropologischen Perspektive werden die Bedürfnisse und Prioritäten ärmerer Menschen ebenso untersucht wie die symbolischen Repräsentationen von Umwelt und die instrumentelle Umweltnutzung. Interessant erscheint in Hinblick auf die zunehmende Bevölkerungsdichte und die stetig schwindenden Flächenressourcen in westafrikanischen Städten, welche Bedeutung einer sauberen Umwelt beigemessen wird.

Stellen die BewohnerInnen der ärmeren, zum Teil informellen Viertel eine Verbindung zwischen der Wohnqualität und dem Umweltschutz her? Wird die Abfall- und Abwasserproblematik im urbanen öffentlichen Raum als Umweltverschmutzung wahrgenommen? Darüber hinaus haben in vielen westafrikanischen Ländern in den vergangenen Jahrzehnten grundlegende Änderungen der Organisation der öffentlichen Verwaltung stattgefunden. Wie haben sich die Dezentralisierungsprozesse, also die Übertragung von organisatorischen und finanziellen Kompetenzen auf die lokalen politischen EntscheidungsträgerInnen, auf die Abfallwirtschaft in den Städten ausgewirkt? Inwiefern werden die Stadtverwaltungen für unterlassene Maßnahmen in der Siedlungshygiene und Abfallwirtschaft von der Bevölkerung zur Rechenschaft gezogen?

Die Forschungsfrage beschränkt sich jedoch nicht nur auf die Analyse des Umweltbewusstseins der ärmeren städtischen Bevölkerung in Westafrika, sondern rückt auch deren Handlungsmöglichkeiten in den Fokus. Die aus dem Mangel an Arbeitsplätzen resultierenden prekären Einkommensverhältnisse sind hierfür höchst bedeutsam, denn sie sind oft der Grund für den fehlenden Zugang zu umweltbezogenen Dienstleistungen und sanitärer Infrastruktur. Welche Prioritäten setzen ärmere Familien, wenn sie über die Verwendung ihrer finanziellen Ressourcen entscheiden? Welche Auswirkungen hat der tatsächliche bzw. der subjektiv empfundene Geldmangel auf die Entsorgung von Abfällen und Abwässern? Und wie reagieren die Menschen auf die Entstehung von wilden Mülldeponien oder die Kontaminierung des Grundwassers?

In der Dissertation wird ein problemzentrierter Ansatz verfolgt, das bedeutet, dass in theoretischer und praktischer Hinsicht sowohl die Vielfalt und Komplexität als auch die Dynamiken der relevanten Phänomene erforscht werden. Die Wahl der Forschungsmethoden stützt sich hauptsächlich auf die Methoden der Kultur- und Sozialanthropologie, welche neue Aspekte aufnehmen und die bisherigen theoretischen Ansätze ergänzen und erweitern können. Anthropologische Ansätze werden aber auch mit anderen sozialwissenschaftlichen Ansätzen und in geringerem Ausmaß auch mit Konzepten aus den Naturwissenschaften und den technischen Wissenschaften ergänzt.

Die Forschung geht von drei unterschiedlichen Annahmen aus: Erstens wird die These überprüft, dass Umweltbewusstsein ein postmaterielles Phänomen ist, welches nur in Industrieländern bzw. unter den gebildeten, wohlhabenden Bevölkerungsschichten in Entwicklungsländern existiert[1]. Hier wird Armut als Ursache von Umweltproblemen gesehen, da die Zielsetzungen und Prioritäten von armen Menschen auf die Verbesserung der ökonomischen Lage und nicht auf die Verbesserung der Umweltqualität fokussiert seien. Zweitens wird die gegenläufige Annahme untersucht, dass Berufsgruppen wie GemüsegärtnerInnen in den Städten des „Globalen Südens" natürliche Ressourcen wie Wasser und Boden nachhaltig nutzen[2]. Dies beruht auf der Annahme, dass die Handlungsweisen von ärmeren Bevölkerungsschichten Lösungen für Umweltprobleme bereitstellen können, weil ärmere Menschen auf die dauerhafte Verfügbarkeit von natürlichen Ressourcen wie Wasser, Ackerflächen und Weideland angewiesen seien. Ein dritter analytischer Ansatz betrachtet Abfall als politisches Protestmittel, das ärmere, marginalisierte StadtbewohnerInnen als bewussten Akt des Widerstands einsetzen[3]. Hier wird erforscht, inwiefern Abfall als politisches Protestmittel gesehen werden kann und die Vermüllung des öffentlichen Raumes eine Reaktion auf mangelnde Mitbestimmungsrechte, Grundstücksspekulationen und Korruption der Stadtverwaltungen ist.

Armut wird in theoretischer Hinsicht sowohl als Mangel an finanziellen Mitteln als auch als Fehlen von Verwirklichungschancen thematisiert[4]. Bei der Bewertung von Armut und der Planung von Maßnahmen zur Armutsminderung beherrschen international vergleichbare statistische Maßzahlen die Diskussion. Gleichzeitig werden nichtökonomische Aspekte von Armut, die sozial und kulturell geprägt sind, ausgeblendet. Die Theorie der Verwirklichungschancen, die von Amartya Sen[5] und Martha Nussbaum[6] geprägt wurde, wird als alternativer Ansatz vorgestellt. Die Freiheit, eigenständige Entscheidungen zu treffen und die Möglichkeit, selbst gesetzte Ziele zu verfolgen, werden hier als zentral erachtet. Dieser Zugang zu Armut erweist sich jedoch vor dem afrikanischen Hintergrund nur als eingeschränkt anwendbar. Einerseits beschränkt sich dieser theoretische Zugang weitgehend auf den Handlungsspielraum von Individuen und andererseits wohnt dem Konzept der Verwirklichungschancen ein gewisser Idealismus inne. Aus diesem Grund werden afrikanische Theorieansätze, die auf Julius Nyerere[7] und Henry Odera Oruka[8] zurückgehen, vorgestellt. Beide Ansätze sind explizit im afrikanischen Kontext entwickelt worden und definieren die Befriedigung von Grundbe-dürfnissen als Voraussetzung für das Anstreben anderer Ziele. Schließlich werden informelle familiäre und nachbarschaftliche Solidaritätsstrategien erörtert, welche Aufschluss über die komplexen Netzwerke der Sozialbeziehungen und die Logik von Unterstützungsleistungen geben.

Umweltverschmutzung und Umweltschutz werden anhand von interdiszipli-nären Zugängen diskutiert und u. a. die Aspekte Vulnerabilität, Gesundheitsge-fährdung und Umweltgerechtigkeit behandelt. Umweltpsychologische Ansätze unterscheiden im Hinblick auf umweltorientiertes Handeln zwischen egoistischen, altruistischen und ökozentrischen Werthaltungen[9]. Inwiefern das Prinzip der Nut-zenmaximierung und das Trittbrettfahrerproblem zur Zerstörung der Umwelt bei-tragen,[10] wird ebenso diskutiert wie Gegenentwürfe, die den sozialen Zusammenhalt in einer Gemeinschaft und interne Regulierungsmechanismen als Lösungsstrate-gien für Umweltkrisen betrachten[11]. Kultur- und sozialanthropologische Ansätze werden herangezogen, um die Parallelen zwischen der Verschmutzung der Umwelt und der Überschreitung von Grenzen im symbolischen Sinn aufzuzeigen[12]. Auf welche Art und Weise Sanktionen erfolgen und der ursprüngliche Zustand durch (symbolische) Reinigung wiederhergestellt werden kann, wird ebenfalls dargelegt. Darüber hinaus wird die Frage nach der Verantwortung bei umweltschädigendem Verhalten gestellt und das Thema Umweltgerechtigkeit angeschnitten. Das Umwelt-bewusstsein der Menschen in westafrikanischen Städten lässt sich nur analysieren, wenn auch kulturelle Vorstellungen in Zusammenhang mit Umweltverschmut-zung[13] berücksichtigt werden. Handlungstheoretische Konzepte erörtern die Rolle von kulturellen Faktoren wie Wissen, Umweltgesetze und Traditionen sowie die Akzeptanz von Umweltmaßnahmen. Im Zusammenspiel mit den Wohn-, Arbeits-und Lebensbedingungen in den Städten und den technischen Gegebenheiten wie der sanitären Infrastruktur werden diese Faktoren gleichzeitig als ermöglichend und einschränkend für das Umwelthandeln gesehen. Handlungsstrategien wurden im Hinblick auf die Umwelt- und Armutsproblematik in den afrikanischen Städten bisher zu wenig Aufmerksamkeit gewidmet, da diese häufig den Gesetzen bzw. den Zielvorgaben von Entwicklungsprojekten entgegenlaufen. Von den Berichten der staatlichen Institutionen oder internationalen Organisationen können keine Ein-blicke in die konkreten Handlungsweisen erwartet werden, denn, sofern sie nicht den Erwartungen entsprechen, werden sie oft als Entwicklungshindernis gesehen. Die kultur- und sozialanthropologische Herangehensweise, welche sich Methoden wie der teilnehmenden Beobachtung und qualitativen Interviews bedient, scheint hier vielversprechend zu sein. Im Hinblick auf meine Forschungsfrage scheint es besonders relevant, die mit Armut einhergehenden Einschränkungen der Hand-lungsfreiheit näher zu bestimmen. Es gilt also der Frage nachzugehen, inwieweit materielle Zwänge, also ökonomische Notwendigkeiten der Bedürfnisbefriedigung, für den Umgang des Menschen mit der Umwelt ausschlaggebend sind.

Der Fokus der Doktorarbeit liegt aufgrund des anthropologischen Zugangs zur Forschungsfrage auf der Analyse des empirischen Datenmaterials. Die Daten-grundlage der qualitativen Erhebungen stützt sich auf ExpertInneninterviews mit einheimischen WissenschaftlerInnen und VertreterInnen von Umweltbehörden, kommunalen Strukturen und (inter-)nationalen Organisationen. Mit Haushalten in zentrumsnahen Stadtvierteln, in Vierteln in städtischer Randlage und in informellen peri-urbanen Siedlungen wurden halbstrukturierte Leitfadeninterviews geführt. Fokusgruppeninterviews mit Frauenvereinigungen und GemüsegärtnerInnen bilden eine wichtige Ergänzung des Datenmaterials. Über siebzig Interviews wurden auf Französisch und der afrikanischen Verkehrssprache Bambara durchgeführt, transkribiert und ausgewertet. Die teilnehmende Beobachtung in Haushalten, in umweltrelevanten Arbeitsfeldern und bei Konferenzen in Bamako und Ouagadougou fließt ebenfalls in die Auswertung und Interpretation der Ergebnisse ein. Diese Daten werden durch aktuelle Statistiken der nationalen Statistikbehörden, aktuelle Gesetzestexte im Bereich Umweltschutz sowie Studien von ForscherInnen nationaler Forschungseinrichtungen in einen größeren Kontext gestellt. Die Forschungskooperation mit dem Dachverband der Kleinunternehmen in der Abfallwirtschaft in Mali gewährte mir schließlich einen Einblick in lokale politische Zusammenhänge und die Bedeutsamkeit der internationalen Entwicklungszusammenarbeit.

Die Forschungsergebnisse zeigen auf, dass ärmere StadtbewohnerInnen oftmals keinen Zugang zu umweltbezogener, kostenpflichtiger Infrastruktur und Dienstleistungen haben. Als Reaktion auf die unzureichende Infrastruktur werden die Kapazitäten der technischen Vorrichtungen überlastet, als Alternative zu teuren Umweltdienstleistungen die Angebote informeller Akteure in Anspruch genommen. Die Kommodifizierung der Entsorgungsleistungen von Abfällen und Abwässern ist ein Prozess, der sich noch im Anfangsstadium befindet und aufgrund der Konkurrenz durch informelle Akteure weder wirtschaftlich noch ökologisch nachhaltig ist. Die Umwelt als soziales Konstrukt beschränkt sich in westafrikanischen Städten auf das unmittelbare Wohnumfeld. Umweltgerechtes Verhalten wird zwar häufig den hygienischen Anforderungen im häuslichen Bereich gerecht, nicht aber der Sauberkeit im öffentlichen Raum. Die Verantwortung für den Umweltschutz wird den staatlichen und kommunalen Verwaltungseinrichtungen sowie internationalen Entwicklungshilfeorganisationen zugeschrieben. Die Unfähigkeit der Stadtverwaltungen, eine funktionierende Abfallwirtschaft sicherzustellen, bedeutet insbesondere für ärmere Familien, die in prekären Wohnverhältnissen leben, dass sie Umweltgefahren ausgesetzt sind. Das „Recht auf die Stadt"[14], als Recht der Partizipation und Aneignung wird ärmeren StadtbewohnerInnen nicht gewährt.

Das Zusammenwirken von fehlender Umweltbildung, wirtschaftlichen Zwangslagen und konsensorientiertem Zusammenleben führt dazu, dass die ärmeren Menschen in den Städten kaum in der Lage sind, ein Umweltbewusstsein zu entwickeln und danach zu handeln. Mangelndes Wissen über die Ursachen für und Folgen von Verschmutzung führt dazu, dass die sanitäre Infrastruktur auf unbeabsichtigte, umweltschädigende Weise genutzt wird. Die unzureichende Befriedigung von (neuen) Grundbedürfnissen ist ausschlaggebend dafür, dass nicht in die umweltgerechte Entsorgung von Abfällen und Abwässern investiert wird. Umweltverschmutzung wird schließlich nicht als mangelndes Verantwortungsbewusstsein im ökologischen Sinn problematisiert, sondern als Verstoß gegen einen nachbarschaftlichen und gemeinschaftlichen Verhaltenskodex. Die Verschmutzung des öffentlichen

Raums durch Abfälle und Abwässer wird häufig weder sozial noch strafrechtlich sanktioniert. Ein anthropozentrisches Umweltverständnis führt dazu, dass Umweltverschmutzung nur bei direkten und unmittelbaren Rückwirkungen auf den Menschen als Problem gesehen wird. Vorsorgendes umweltorientiertes Handeln hat für ärmere StadtbewohnerInnen nicht die höchste Priorität.

Die Doktorarbeit präsentiert Lösungsvorschläge, die sowohl auf die strukturellen Handlungsbedingungen als auch auf die Motivationen für umweltadäquates Handeln eingehen. Sozial gestaffelte Tarife für die Inanspruchnahme von Dienstleistungen der Abfall- und Abwasserentsorgung könnten dazu beitragen, die Verschmutzung des öffentlichen Raumes einzudämmen. Ärmere StadtbewohnerInnen würden dann vermutlich weniger auf informelle AbfallsammlerInnen zurückgreifen, um sich der Haushaltsabfälle zu entledigen. Umweltbildungsmaßnahmen, die von angesehenen lokalen Persönlichkeiten durchgeführt werden, könnten sich günstig auf das umweltrelevante Verhalten der ärmeren Bevölkerungsschichten auswirken. Die Einführung von Mechanismen, die es ärmeren StadtbewohnerInnen ermöglichen, politische Entscheidungen zu beeinflussen, wird als notwendig erachtet.

Anmerkungen

1   Vgl. Diekmann, Andreas/Franzen, Axel (1999): *The Wealth of Nations and Environmental Concern.* In: Environment and Behavior, 31 (4), S. 540–549; Inglehart, Ronald (1995): *Public Support for Environmental Protection: Objective Problems and Subjective Values in 43 Societies.* In: Political Science and Politics, 28 (1), S. 57–72.

2   Vgl. Guha, Ramachandra/Martinez-Alier, Joan (1997): *Varieties of Environmentalism: Essays North and South.* London: Earthscan; Martinez-Alier, Joan (2002): *The Environmentalism of the Poor. A Study of Ecological Conflicts and Valuation.* Cheltenham: Edward Elgar.

3   Vgl. Bouju, Jacky (2009): *Urban Dwellers, Politicians and Dirt: An Anthropology of Everyday Governance in Bobo-Dioulasso (Burkina Faso).* In: Blundo, Giorgio/Le Meur, Pierre-Yves (Hrsg.): The Governance of Daily Life in Africa: Ethnographic Explorations of Public and Collective Services. Leiden/Boston: Brill, S. 143–170; Fredericks, Rosalind C. (2009): *Doing the Dirty Work: The Cultural Politics of Garbage Collection in Dakar, Senegal.* Dissertation. Berkeley: University of California.

4   Vgl. Sen, Amartya K. (2002): *Ökonomie für den Menschen. Wege zu Gerechtigkeit und Solidarität in der Marktwirtschaft.* München: Deutscher Taschenbuch Verlag.

5   Ebd.

6   Nussbaum, Martha (2006): *Poverty and Human Functioning: Capabilities as Fundamental Entitlements.* In Grusky, David/Kanbur, Ravi (Hrsg.): Poverty and inequality. Stanford: Stanford University Press, S. 47–75.

7   Nyerere, Julius K. (1973): *Freedom and Development. A Selection From Writings and Speeches 1968–1973.* Dar Es Salaam: Oxford University Press.

8   Oruka, Henry Odera (1997): *Six Liberties.* In: Graneß, Anke/Kresse, Kai (Hrsg.): Sagacious Reasoning. Henry Odera Oruka in Memoriam. Frankfurt am Main: Lang, S. 47–59.

9   Vgl. De Groot, Judith/Steg, Linda (2008): *Value Orientations to Explain Beliefs Related to Environmental Significant Behavior. How to Measure Egoistic, Altruistic, and Biospheric Value Orientations.* In: Environment and Behavior, 40 (3), S. 330–354.

10 Vgl. Hardin, Garrett (1968): *The Tragedy of the Commons.* In: Science, 162 (3859), S. 1243–1248.

11 Vgl. Ostrom, Elinor (1990): *Governing the Commons: The Evolution of Institutions for Collective Action.* Cambridge: Cambridge University Press.

12 Vgl. Douglas, Mary (2003[1966]): *Purity and Danger. An Analysis of Concepts of Pollution and Taboo. Collected Works. Volume II.* London: Routledge.

13 Vgl. Chevron, Marie-France (2002): *Ethnische Zugehörigkeit, Lebensweise und Umweltverhalten in den Städten von Mali.* In Chevron, Marie-France/Reinprecht, Christoph/Traoré, Gaoussou (Hrsg.): Umwelt und Urbanität in Westafrika. Beiträge zur Müllverwertung und Abfallproblematik. Frankfurt am Main: Brandes & Apsel/Südwind, S. 114 –128.

14 Lefebvre, Henri (1968): *Le droit à la ville.* Paris: Editions Anthropos.

Lorenz Probst

Drivers and constraints of an innovation towards improved vegetable safety in urban West Africa (Benin, Ghana and Burkina Faso)

Anhaltende Urbanisierungsprozesse und eine Veränderung der Ernährungsge-wohnheiten haben zu steigender Nachfrage nach Gemüse in Cotonou, Accra und Ouagadougou geführt. Bäuerinnen und Bauern reagieren auf diese Nachfrage des lokalen Marktes, indem sie auf unverbauten Flächen und abhängig von der Verfüg-barkeit von Bewässerungsquellen Gemüse produzieren. Gleichzeitig hat die Bedeu-tung der Außer-Haus-Verpflegung, welche auch Gemüse aus urbaner Produktion verarbeitet, zugenommen. Aufgrund der Verwendung verunreinigten Wassers zur Bewässerung, aufgrund der Verschmutzung der Umwelt sowie aufgrund der ris-kanten Verwendung synthetischer Pestizide ist die Produktion von Gemüse in den genannten Städten sozial und ökologisch nicht nachhaltig. Dies macht die Notwen-digkeit einer Innovation hin zu gesünderen und nachhaltigeren Anbaumethoden deutlich; eine solche Innovation würde sowohl Bäuerinnen und Bauern, als auch KonsumentInnen und der Umwelt zugutekommen.

Das Ziel dieser Arbeit war es, zu einem besseren Verständnis von Faktoren beizutragen, welche eine solche Innovation fördern oder hemmen. Das Haupt-gewicht wurde dabei auf Pflanzenschutz-Strategien und Pestizidverwendung gelegt. Im Einzelnen untersuchte die Arbeit (1) Faktoren, welche die Veränderung von Anbaumethoden auf Farmebene antreiben oder hemmen; erforschte (2) das Potenzial, zertifiziertes Gemüse aus ökologischer Landwirtschaft über den Sektor der Außer-Haus-Verpflegung zu vermarkten; etablierte (3) einen Lernprozess von Stakeholdern des Innovationssystems, um innovationsfördernde und -hemmende Faktoren zu erarbeiten und zu diskutieren. Dementsprechend positioniert sich die Arbeit theoretisch in Konzepten landwirtschaftlicher Innovationssysteme, setzt aber auch die Sub-Konzepte der Wertschöpfungskette und der Verbraucherent-scheidung ein.

Um die genannten Forschungsziele zu erreichen, wurden in Cotonou, Accra und Ouagadougou empirische Daten erhoben. Auf Ebene der Produktionsstätten wurde eine partizipative Fallstudie mit 106 TeilnehmerInnen durchgeführt, in der Methoden des Participatory Rural Appraisal und qualitative empirische Methoden kombiniert wurden. Im Sektor der Außer-Haus-Verpflegung wurden Verkäufe-rInnen ($n = 180$) und KonsumentInnen ($n = 360$) zu Verwendung von Gemüse, Risikowahrnehmung, Kaufentscheidung und Zahlungswilligkeit für ökologische

Zertifizierung befragt. Schließlich wurde ein partizipativer Lernprozess organisiert, zu dem Akteure des gesamten Innovationssystems eingeladen wurden.

Das gegenwärtige System zur Produktion und Vermarktung von Gemüse fördert nicht-nachhaltige und riskante Anbaupraktiken, und hat sich bisher gegenüber Vorschlägen einer Veränderung hin zu gesünderen und nachhaltigeren Anbaumethoden resistent verhalten. Die Verhaltensmuster von Bäuerinnen und Bauern wurden durch verschiedene Faktoren beeinflusst: inhärente Faktoren, welche Verhaltensalternativen charakterisieren; verstärkende Faktoren wie Nachfrage und politische Rahmensetzung; Mobilitätsfaktoren welche Bäuerinnen und Bauern befähigen, sich hin zu alternativen Strategien zu „bewegen"; sowie Zugangsfaktoren welche den Zugang von Bäuerinnen und Bauern zu relevantem Wissen charakterisieren.

Diese Ergebnisse unterstreichen die Bedeutung der Interaktion mit verschiedensten Akteuren als eine Voraussetzung für Veränderungsprozesse hin zu gesünderen und nachhaltigeren Anbaumethoden.

Bezüglich des Potenzials zur Vermarktung zertifizierten Gemüses aus ökologischer Landwirtschaft über die Außer-Haus-Verpflegung ergab sich, dass das Bewusstsein über eine chemische Kontamination niedrig war. Die Kaufentscheidung beim Gemüsekauf durch VerkäuferInnen in der Außer-Haus-Verpflegung wurde vor allem vom Aussehen (etwa Frische und Farbe) beeinflusst, während KonsumentInnen ökologischer Zertifizierung und Geschmack ähnlichen Nutzen zusprachen. Die Zahlungswilligkeit für ökologische Zertifizierung betrug im Schnitt 0,848 USD für einen Korb mit 3 kg frischen Tomaten (VerkäuferInnen), – dies entspricht einem Aufschlag von 12 % bis 53 %, abhängig von Jahreszeit und Land. Die Zahlungswilligkeit für ökologische Zertifizierung von Gemüse in einer Mahlzeit betrug im Schnitt 1,044 USD pro Teller (KonsumentInnen) – dies entspricht einem Aufschlag von 19 % in Restaurants.

Im Bereich praktische Anwendung und politische Rahmensetzung zieht die Arbeit den Schluss, dass die individuelle und kollektive Verantwortung für notwendige Veränderung ebenso wie die Veränderungskompetenz von Bäuerin und Bauer unterstrichen und gestärkt werden muss. Dies kann erreicht werden durch das Fördern von kollektivem Handeln und die Stärkung von Gruppenidentität; durch eine Investition in die Bildung und Ausbildung von Bäuerinnen und Bauern; durch die Stärkung des finanziellen, physischen, sozialen und natürlichen Kapitals von Bäuerinnen und Bauern; durch das Einrichten von Multi-Stakeholder Plattformen, um Lernprozesse zu verstärken; durch eine Reform des Marktes für Pestizide sowie durch die Förderung von Marktnachfrage nach „risikoreduzierten" Produkten.

Auf der konzeptuellen Ebene erwies sich das Konzept landwirtschaftlicher Innovationssysteme und die eingefügten Sub-Konzepte und Methoden als nützlich um Faktoren zu verstehen, welche zu einer Innovation beitragen oder diese hemmen können.

Zukünftige Forschung sollte die Produktion und den Konsum von Gemüse nach Sorte und Verkaufsort systematisch aufzeichnen und Untersuchungen zu Pestizidrückständen durchführen. So könnten überzeugende Botschaften bezüglich tatsächlicher Risiken für KonsumentInnen an die Politik formuliert werden. Außerdem sollte das gegenwärtig populäre Interventionsinstrument der Multi-Stakeholder

Plattform kritisch hinterfragt werden bezüglich der Fragen, ob solche Plattformen kommunikative Rationalitäten schaffen können, und wie solche Plattformen auf Macht- und Wissensunterschiede zwischen Stakeholdern einwirken beziehungsweise von diesen Unterschieden beeinflusst werden. Schließlich sollte untersucht werden, inwiefern kommunikative Rationalität im Besonderen zu Innovationen hin zu nachhaltigen landwirtschaftlichen Praktiken beitragen kann.

Autorinnen und Autoren

Gerhard Adam, Bakk.phil. MA, geboren 1985 in der Steiermark, studierte und arbeitete zwei Jahre in Mexiko und Spanien, wo er seine Masterarbeit zum Thema Menschenrechte und Wasserkraft in Mexiko verfasste. Er arbeitete als Studienassistent am Institut für Wirtschafts-, Sozial- und Unternehmensgeschichte an der Universität Graz, wo er auch das Masterstudium der Global Studies absolvierte. Im Zuge eines mehrmonatigen Forschungsaufenthalts in Bhutan entstand seine Masterarbeit zu nachhaltigem Tourismus und Entwicklung in Bhutan. Seit Mai 2013 arbeitet Adam bei Südwind Steiermark. Er ist Regionalstellenleiter und Leiter von DEAR-Programmen der Europäischen Kommission zu Global Citizenship Education bzw. Globalem Lernen.
Gerhard.Adam@gmx.net

Robert Hafner, PhD, geboren 1985 in Mittersill, absolvierte seinen BA in European Studies an der Malmö University (Schweden), studierte an der Roskilde University (Dänemark) und der Universidad de León (Spanien), bevor er seinen MSc und PhD in Geographie an der Universität Innsbruck abschloss. Neben unzähligen längeren Forschungsaufenthalten in Argentinien (unter anderem zu den Themenfeldern Abfall, Umweltgerechtigkeit und Soja-Agrobusiness) entwickelte er die von Viskeralität beeinflusste Jazz Methodologie. Derzeit forscht und publiziert er im Rahmen des Post-DocTrack-Pilotprogramms der ÖAW.
Robert.Hafner@uibk.ac.at

Dr. Elisabeth Huber, geboren 1983 in Klagenfurt, studierte Kultur- und Sozialanthropologie sowie Soziologie an der Universität Wien. 2017 schloss sie ihre Dissertation zum Thema Armut und umweltgerechtes Handeln in westafrikanischen Städten ab. Studien- und Forschungsaufenthalte führten sie nach Frankreich sowie nach Mali und Burkina Faso. Von 2017 bis 2018 war sie wissenschaftliche Mitarbeiterin im EU H2020-Projekt „Knowledge Complexity" am Institut für Sozial- und Kulturanthropologie der Freien Universität Berlin. Seit Mai 2018 ist sie für das Forschungsdatenmanagement im SFB „Affective Societies" an der FU Berlin tätig.
e.huber@fu-berlin.de

Maria Katelieva, MA, geboren 1986 in Dobritsch, Bulgarien, studierte Tourismusmanagement sowie Kultur- und Sozialanthropologie an den Universitäten Sofia (Bulgarien) und Wien. Sie arbeitet als wissenschaftliche Mitarbeiterin an der IMC FH Krems und zu ihren Forschungsschwerpunkten zählen nachhaltige Tourismus-

und Regionalentwicklung, kulturelle und soziale Aspekte des Tourismus, sowie qualitative Forschungsmethoden. Derzeit arbeitet sie an ihrer Dissertation zum Thema Inwertsetzung und Schutz von traditionellem Wissen als Teil des immateriellen Kulturerbes.

Maria.Katelieva@fh-krems.ac.at

Dr. Johannes Knierzinger, geboren 1981 in Grieskirchen, ist Postdoktorand am Institut de recherche pour le développement (IRD) und Mitglied der Forschungseinheit UMR PRODIG (CNRS) in Paris, wo er gegenwärtig zu den soziopolitischen Folgen von Minenschließungen in Westafrika forscht. Zudem arbeitet er derzeit an einer weiteren Monographie, in der er die Rohstoffkrisen der 2000er Jahre aus einem historischen Blickwinkel betrachtet. Seine Dissertation wurde 2018 von Palgrave Macmillan als Teil der International Political Economy Series publiziert.

johannes.knierzinger@univie.ac.at

Univ.-Doz. Mag. Dr. Andreas J. Obrecht, geboren 1961 in Wien, studierte Sozial- und Kulturanthropologie sowie Soziologie an der Universität Wien. In 30 Jahren universitärer Lehre führte er u. a. Forschungen in Melanesien, Subsahara-Afrika und Südostasien durch und ist seit 2009 Leiter der Geschäftsstelle der „Kommission für Entwicklungsforschung" (www.kef-research.at) und Leiter des „Austrian Partnership Programme in Higher Education and Research for Development" (www.appear.at). Zudem hat er zahlreiche Artikel und wissenschaftliche Werke veröffentlicht und rund 400 wissenschafts- und kulturpublizistische Live-Sendungen für ORF Ö1 moderiert.

Andreas.Obrecht@oead.at

Dr. Mag. Lorenz Probst, geboren 1982 in München, ist Deputy Director des Centre for Development Research an der Universität für Bodenkultur Wien. Seine Leidenschaft ist das Gestalten, Begleiten und Analysieren von Lernprozessen im Bereich nachhaltiger Entwicklung. Diese Leidenschaft bringt Lorenz Probst in Forschungs-, Lehr- und Kooperationsprojekten in Afrika, Südostasien, Lateinamerika und Europa ein. Wissenschaftlich setzt er sich momentan mit transformativem Lernen und kommunikativem Handeln in Nachhaltigkeitstransitionen auseinander.

lorenz.probst@boku.ac.at

Salomé Ritterband, MA, geboren 1991 in London, GB, verbrachte ihre Kindheit in London, Buenos Aires und Wien. Die Auslandsschweizerin schloss ihr Studium in Kultur- und Sozialanthropologie an der Universität Wien ab. Der Beitrag in diesem Band basiert auf der mittlerweile publizierten Masterarbeit, wofür Salomé Ritterband 2017 den Österreichischen Nachwuchspreis für Entwicklungsforschung

erhielt. Salomé Ritterband arbeitete viele Jahre als Kostümassistentin und Kom-
parsin an verschiedenen Theatern in Wien und ist heute als Kulturvermittlerin im
Weltmuseum Wien tätig.
salome.ritterband@hotmail.com

Weitere Bände der Reihe „Schriftenreihe der OeAD-GmbH":

Ernst Gesslbauer, Carin Dániel Ramírez-Schiller, Lydia Rössler (Hrsg.)
Auslandserfahrung und duale Ausbildung – Praxis und Potenzial

Band 1
100 Seiten € 16,90, kartoniert mit Farbabbildungen
ISBN 978-3-7065-5120-5

Michael Dippelreiter, Hubert Dürrstein (Hrsg.)
50 Jahre Bildungsmobilität
Eine kleine Geschichte des OeAD

Band 2
128 Seiten, € 18,90, kartoniert mit zahlreichen s/w-Abbildungen
ISBN 978-3-7065-5128-1

Ernst Gesslbauer, Gerhard Volz, Magdalena Burtscher (Hrsg.)
Mit Erasmus durch Europa
Österreichische Studierende berichten über ihren Auslandsaufenthalt. Eine Studie

Band 3
152 Seiten, € 21,90, kartoniert mit vielen Farbabbildungen und Grafiken
ISBN 978-3-7065-5173-1

Andreas J. Obrecht (Hrsg.)
Wissen und Entwicklung
30 Jahre Kommission für Entwicklungsfragen (KEF). Ein Reader zu Wissensproduktion und Entwicklungsforschung

Band 4
224 Seiten, € 24,90, kartoniert mit Farb- und s/w-Abbildungen
ISBN 978-3-7065-5228-8

Ernst Gesslbauer, Ursula Großruck, Petra Siegele (Hrsg.)
Schule grenzenlos
Erfahrungen und Herausforderungen im 21. Jahrhundert

Band 5
144 Seiten, € 21,90, kartoniert mit zahlreichen Farbabbildungen
ISBN 978-3-7065-5229-5

Andreas J. Obrecht (Hrsg.)
Wissen und Entwicklung II
Ein Reader zu Theorie und Empirie in der Entwicklungsforschung. Texte zum
Nachwuchspreis der Kommission für Entwicklungsforschung (KEF)

Band 6
84 Seiten, € 21,90, kartoniert mit vielen Farb- und s/w-Abbildungen
ISBN 978-3-7065-5380-3

Ernst Gesslbauer, Carin Dániel Ramírez-Schiller (Hrsg.)
Die Rolle von Guidance in einer sich wandelnden Arbeitswelt

Band 7
144 Seiten, € 21,90, kartoniert mit Farb- und s/w-Abbildungen
ISBN 978-3-7065-5426-8

Stefan Zotti (Hrsg.)
International Lectures
22 Beiträge zur Internationalisierung der Hochschulen

Band 8
118 Seiten, € 17,90, kartoniert mit s/w-Abbildungen
978-3-7065-5600-2
